JEWISH SPAIN
A Guide

JEWISH SPAIN
A Guide

by
MANUEL AGUILAR
and
IAN ROBERTSON

altalena

© Manuel Aguilar & Ian Robertson   1984
Altalena Editores S A
Cochabamba 2
Madrid 16
First Printing   April 1984
ISBN   84-7475-165-9
Deposito legal: M-13531-1984
Phototypesetting by Comphoto Nicolas Morales 38-40 Madrid 19
Printed in Spain by
Graficas Roanca Molina Seca 13 Fuenlabrada Madrid

PREFACE

This is the first Guide published in English devoted entirely to the sites and monuments still existing in peninsular Spain and the Balearic Islands of specific interest to Jewry. Other guides in other languages have covered various aspects of the large subject, but too often they extended their pages with descriptions of places which offer hardly any remains of interest to the present-day visitor, or merely speculate on the possible but unsubstantiated site of a synagogue or judería, etc.

Admittedly the subject is highly elusive. Even when it is possible to identify the location of a Judería, there is non little in it which is specifically Jewish: even those synagogues that have survived through the intervening centuries were built by non-Jewish architects and artisans, while most of the tombstones from Jewish cemeteries can only now be seen in museums, and many are distant from their original sites. The latter funerary inscriptions are probably the most tangible objects remaining, alas; apart from the more abstract expressions of Jewish culture still extant from fifteen centuries of Jewish history in Spain: those monumental work of philosophy, religion, poetry, and science, which are her inestimable heritage. A heritage which while remaining peculiarly Jewish is marked with the imprint of the land whe Jews lived and worked for centuries; a heritage that has become the heritage of our modern culture.

A brief historical introduction has been written, which attempts to provide the necessary chronological framework; while a selective Bibliography *has been compiled containing a number of books on various aspects of Jewish Spain, many of which will contain bibliographies for further or more*

1

specialised reading. A Glossary has also been provided, which it is hoped will be sufficient to explain some terms, not all of which are generally familiar.

It should be emphasised that this guide does not set out to describe any other than Jewish sites and monuments in Spain, although some may be mentioned in passing, for which the discriminating traveller is advised to acquire the English Blue Guide to Spain *(published by Ernest Benn, Ltd, London; and by W.W. Norton & Co. Inc., New York), which covers them in considerable detail.*

The bulk of this volume is devoted to concise descriptions of the more important towns in Spain (and including Ceuta) in which there were Jewish communities. Some of these have been provided with a plan, and they have been set out in alphabetical order. This section has been followed by appendices giving further information with regard to other towns with a Jewish past but without present remains; to eminent Jews; and to addresses of Jewish organisations in contemporary Spain.

Most of the descriptions have been written in the light of personal observation on the spot by the editors during recent extensive tours of the country in the service of the Guide. No one is better aware of the difficulty —particularly in a first edition— of avoiding errors of omission and commission, especially in an area of research which has received comparatively little systematic study, and constructive suggestions for its improvement are solicited.

INTRODUCTION

The Jews in Spanish History

This brief introduction does not attempt to do more than place the Spanish Jews in their historical context — it is not a history of medieval Spain, nor of the Jews in the peninsula as a whole, both having been the subject of numerous comprehensive studies in English, Spanish, and other languages, a selective list of which will be found on p.17.

The problems of co-existence between the three great faiths of the peninsula —Muslim, Christian, and Jewish— «people of the book», that is monotheists with written scriptures, lay at the heart of the racial and religious persecution in medieval Spain. Although certain Christian rulers referred to themselves as being «king of the three religions» —indeed they considered the Jews as their own property— they were unable in an increasingly intolerant age in Europe to delay indefinitely the eventual expulsion of the unconverted Jews, which happened to coincide with the virtual termination of the reconquest of Muslim-occupied Andalucía, or *al-Andalus,* in 1492, and with the discovery of America. It is worth noting that the Jewish minority had been tolerated in Spain for longer than by some other nations: the expulsion of the Jews from England, for example, had been decreed 200 years earlier, in 1290; while those of France were expelled in 1306, and those of Geneva in 1490. There is evidence thet many moved into Navarre and elsewhere in Christian Spain, some having emigrated in the mid 13C. Basically, it was the refusal of the old order to accept the growing importance of a section of the urban community which controlled its capital and commerce; their conversion or dispersion was considered axiomatic by the ecclesiastical aristocracy: not that the edict of 1492 solved the problem.

Our knowledge of Jewish settlement in the Romanised Iberian peninsula prior to the Muslim invasion of 711 CE is slight. Following Phoenician or Greek trading routes the first Jewish traders or settlers may have arrived directly from the Holy Land or Alexandria after coasting along the Mediterranean shores, or via Rome, and small colonies were established in the Balearic Islands, at such ports as Barcelona, Tarragona, Tortosa, Mahón, and Sagunto, and further south, as confirmed by a number of inscriptions on tombstones —such as that of the 3C at Adra (ancient Abdera)— and sarcophagi. One, from Tarragona —now in the Sephardic Museum of Toledo—, reads: «Peace be on Israel and on us and on our children, Amen»; and there are references to the daughter of a rabbi of Tortosa, and of an *archisynagogus* at Elche. They later made their way up the valleys of the great rivers —up the Guadalquivir to Córdoba, and up the Ebro from Tortosa to Zaragoza and the Rioja. Some colonies are known to have existed in the Duero valley and along the southern slopes of the Pyrenees.

At Elvira, near present-day Granada, a Church Council deliberated c.314 on a variety of ecclesiastical problems, some with specific written reference —and the first of such— to relations between Christians and Jews, in which it was implied that some Jews also owned land or were agriculturalists: it also included certain restrictive clauses. From this date until about 430 there was a constant struggle between the two faiths to convert the Hispani to their respective religions, each vying for proselytes.

During the period of Visigothic rule in the peninsula the Jews were able, in general, to carry out their trading and other activities with comparatively little interference; indeed commerce was largely in their hands, or of foreigners, with the consequence that when economic recessions set in, Jews were blamed; but any antiJewish legislation which followed led only to further disruptions in trade. Early in the 5C, excited by **Sever,** there had been an attack on the Jewish community of Mahón (Minorca), whose synagogue was destroyed, and some 540 Jews were compelled to accept baptism, whereby becoming in fact the first *conversos*, although the term did not come into general use until the late 14C.

In 589, at the Third Council of Toledo, **Reccared,** having recently renounced Arianism, enforced Roman Catholicism on the kingdom, but still the Jews enjoyed tolerance, although they could not have Christian slaves, nor hold public office. They could however, and did, take up the profession of tax-farmers, even at that early period, an unpopular and dangerous occupation for which Christians didn't offer themselves as candidates. Some Jews were attracted to Toledo, the Visigothic capital; others settled in smaller towns away from the seats of administration.

During the reigns of **Sisebut** and **Sisenand** (early 7C) further royal decrees were promulgated. Jews should not be converted by force, but penalties were established for any who relapsed and resumed their former faith; Jews with Christian wives were to be converted and their children would be baptised as Christians; those who accepted conversion might not consort whith their previous co-religionists. Fewer Jews now openly confessed their faith. In 688 **Egica** became king. He was apparently convinced that there was a Jewish conspiracy, and that they were planning an uprising against the Christians; and among his discrimatory legislations (at the 17th Council of Toledo, in 694) was a decree ordering that Jewish merchant colonies be removed from the south and east coasts of Spain. But far more dangerous was the growing power and expansion of the Muslims since the death of the prophet Mohammed in 632; and it has been suggested that they may well have been encouraged to invade Spain by the Jews of North Africa; indeed **Tariq**, the leader of the expeditionary force, may himself have been a Jew.

The invasion came in 711. Tariq landed near Gibraltar, decisively defeated the Visigoth army at the battle of the Guadalete, and wintered in Toledo, which it is said was virtually abandoned except for the Jews. The keys of this city, together with those of Córdoba, Elvira, and Seville, in the absence of Christians, were entrusted to leaders of the Jewish communities who offered few risks, and who had welcomed them. The conquest was primarily a military occupation.

In 756, **Abderrahman,** sole survivor of the Ommayad dynasty at Damascus, obtained recognition of his independent emirate, but it was not until the reign of **Abderrahman III** (912-61) that any semblance of unity was established. The Muslims at first had neither the resources nor the wish to undertake the management of the Christian or Jewish communities, which as *dhimmis* or «protected persons» enjoyed considerable toleration, although they were excluded from owning land by prohibitive taxation. Together with the *Mozarabs,* the Hispano-Romans who had not converted to Islam (as oposed to the *Muwallads* —or *Muladíes* in Spanish— who converted to Islam) they formed substantial minorities in the larger cities such as Córdoba, Zaragoza, Granada, Seville, and Toledo. The former, particularly under Abderraham's son **al-Hakam** II, became a sophisticated centre of learning under the leadership of the aristocratic rabbi **Hasdai ibn Shaprut** (c.915-c.969), who served as vizier, physician, and diplomat to the Caliphate. The Caliph sent Hasdai to the Christian king Sancho the Fat to cure him of his ailment, and the success of his treatment brought him the overlordship of five towns. He was also the spokesman for all Western Jews in resolving the question as to whether the kingdom of the Khazars was in fact *the* Jewish Kingdom.

By 1000 CE Jews had become largely arabised in culture throughout the Islamic world, participating extensively in the composition of Judeo-Arabic poetry, both this and much of Jewish philosophy and scientific scholarship being set down in Arabic written in Hebrew characters. The Jews, often trilingual, collaborated in the translation of astronomical, mathematical, and other scientific works, etc. from Arabic into Latin. The medical treatise of **Ibn Zuhr**, the «Taysír», was known to Barcelona Jews in 1165, four years after the author's death, although it was not known to Spanish Christians until 1281. Cosmopolitan Toledo was likewise a centre of translation, in which the Jewish community flourished, although on its capture in 1085 the indigenous Mozarab population was entirely Arab-speaking.

Occasionally, but this was rare, Jews were put in positions of considerable authority: for example two members of the **Ibn Nagrella** family, Samuel and Joseph, served the Berber rulers as viziers in Granada — then known as «Gharnata-Yahud» («of the Jews»), but the main reason for this was to remove any control of the city from the hands of the previous Arab regime. In general the Berber influence, from the *Almoravide* invasion towards the end of the 11C, and more so after the irruption of the more fanatical *Almohades* in 1147, was decidedly unfavourable to the Jews of al-Andalus, for there were frequent acts of repression against non-Muslims — as at Lucena. These caused two waves of Jewish migration to that growing area meanwhile reconquered by the Christians — in 1085 (the year Toledo fell to them), and again in 1148. Already during this period of insecurity, in 1140, a Jewish merchant of Fez, writing to his father in Almería, warned him of the anti-Jewish feeling «rampant in this country to a degree that, in comparison with it, Almería is a place of salvation».

Among the more eminent Jews in al-Andalus at this period may be mentioned: the philosophers **Salomon ibn Gabirol**, also known as **Avicebron** (c.1021-c.1057; born in Málaga), whose *Fons Vitae* was to be a keystone in medieval Christian scholastic thought; **Moses Maimonides** (1135-1204; born in Córdoba); the poet, **Moses ibn Ezra** (c.1055-c.1138; born en Granada) and **Yehudah Halevi** (c.1075-c.1140; born in Tudela).

Meanwhile, in the north of the peninsula, ever since the symbolic victory of **Pelayo** at Covadonga in 718 (in which a small probing force of Moors were repulsed), the Christian kingdoms had been pushing slowly south from the Asturias, Navarre, and their Pyrenean strongholds, although they occasionally suffered setbacks, particularly during the reign of **Hisham II** (976-1013), whose powerful minister **Almansor** frequently indulged in summer campaigns or *aceifas*, in which he ravaged Barcelona, León, and even Compostela. Taking advantage of the anarchy which later set in among the petty independent Arab states or *taifas*, often themselves distracted by civil wars, the Christian rulers of León, Castile, Navarre, Aragón, and Catalonia kept up an inexorable pressure on the Muslims, who were often obliged to pay tribute to them. Eventually the latter turned to North Africa for aid, the result being a second invasion of al-Andalus by the Almorávides, followed by the Almohades.

The Jews in the Christian north, with their agricultural, artisanal, and commercial interests, appear to have lived a reasonably peaceful life among a warlike and —compared to the south— an uncultured and largely illiterate population of peasants and knights unaccustomed to feudal order such as existed in France. Petty jealousy exposed them to occasional indiscriminate attack, even from the French crusaders, less tolerant than the Spanish nobility, for the latter often profited by protecting the community. Naturally, with the gradual growth of the middle classes, there were rivalries and tensions, for the Jews in general had a higher literacy rate and often a wider cultural horizon than the Christians, playing a significant role in medieval Spain far out of proportion to their numbers, and this was accentuated as they increased their power by concentrating on their traditional activities in the field of finance. Medieval custom and religious laws frowned on the lending of money at usury, or at interest, to a co-religionist (both among Jews, and among Christians), and the latter, at all levels —kings, prelates, the nobility, and the man in the street— appear to have been perennially in need of funds, and could *only* recourse to Jews, who, more experienced, were often more astute and efficient bankers and tax-farmers than themselves.

The interest on such loans was usually high, but not more so than was usual at the period, even if they now appear excessive, for the risks were correspondingly high. In 1081 pressure had been brought to bear on the Pope himself to warn Alfonso VI of Castile not to appoint Jews to positions of authority over Christians, but in spite of protests from religious zealots, among others —for *envidia* or envy was (and some would say still is) a deep-seated vice among the indigenous Spaniards— the Jews continued to serve as tax-collectors. Although the stereotype was set as early as the mid 12C, as confirmed by the *Cid's* transaction with the Jews of Burgos, it was not until the 14C that it became pronouncedly a Jewish activity in Castile, who thus played a central role in the fiscal system, although the community was as equally involved in other commercial, industrial, and cultural activities.

Uncontestably, numerous abuses occurred in the field of usury, which made the Jews particularly susceptible to popular hostility, specially in times of economic crises, and they were liable to experience anti-semitic reactions both in Muslim Spain — with attacks on the *aljamas* (or *juderías*) of Córdoba (1013, and again in 1135), Zaragoza (1039), Granada (1066), and Valencia (1144-45) and in Christian Spain, when restrictions were imposed on them after the depressions of the 12C, and again in 1275, while the anti-Jewish depositions of the *Cortes* in 1301 and 1307 were likewise precipitated by economic recessions.

Although the Jews were among the pioneer settlers in territories reconquered by the Christians, and were granted certain privileges — for the kings required secretaries proficient in Arabic to assist with administration, etc., nevertheless they were still considered in low esteem by the dominant majority, and discriminated against.

In some *fueros,* or charters, for example, murder was considered a capital crime for Muslims and Jews, but Christians were only subjected to a fine. On the whole, Jews were deemed to be the property of the kings who insured their safety and often inherited their property. Partly on account of legislation, but also as a form of self-defence, the urban Jews would congregate in a sector of the town known as the *judería*, just as the Arab or Mudéjar population remained in their *morerías*.

Although **Alfonso VIII** of Castile had been defeated by the Almohades at *Alarcos* in 1195, the Christian reconquest continued to gain ground. In 1118 **Alfonso I** of Aragón, el Batallador, entered Zaragoza, and later captured Tarazona, Calatayud, and Daroca; while Lérida and Tortosa fell to Ramón Berenguer IV; but the battle that crippled the Muslims in al-Andalus was that of *Las Navas de Tolosa* (in 1212; between the Pass of Despeñaperros and Bailén), in which Alfonso VIII was allied with the kings of León, Aragón, and Navarre. Castile was finally united with León in the person of **Fernando III**, to whom in 1236 Córdoba fell; in 1241, Murcia; and in 1248, Sevilla; he is buried in Seville Cathedral in a silver casket showing an epitaph in Latin, Arabic, and Hebrew. Concurrently, **Jaime I** of Aragón, el Conquistador, gained control of the Balearics in 1229, and regained Valencia in 1238; and by 1266 Alicante was in his hands.

The Muslim *Nasrid* dynasty still retained much of what is now Andalucía, but the history of Castile from the death of Fernando III (1252) to the accession of the Catholic Kings (1474: **Fernando V** of Aragón and **Isabel I** of Castile) being one long period of civil war, they were left in comparative peace. But the reconquests of the 13C had destroyed racial co-existence in the peninsula, and a consciousness of conflicting interests came to the fore together with an increasing awareness of the potential dangers —both religious and racial— which were presented by the still considerable Moorish and Jewish minorities, for the latter formed the most dynamic section of the urban middle class.

At Rome, in 1215, the *Fourth Lateran Council* called for further anti-Jewish legislation, but the order that Jews should wear a distinguishing patch on their clothing promulgated at the Council of Arles in 1235 was not to any extent enforced in Spain until c.1480, although approved in principle at the *Cortes of Toro* in 1371. Meanwhile, the *Cortes of Valladolid* in 1293 had formulated other repressive decrees. During the civil war between **Pedro I**, the Cruel and **Enrique de Trastámara**, which had ended at *Montiel* two years previously, the latter had accused Pedro of being merely a puppet in Jewish hands. Indeed, his counsellor and treasurer was Samuel Halevi, who erected the *Tránsito* synagogue in Toledo which engendered some anti-semitic rioting in the following decade; likewise the Jews were held responsible for the outbreak in Spain of the epidemic known as the Black Death (1348); but it was not until June 1391 that the first serious massacres occurred, spurred on by the religious fanaticism of **Ferrant Martínez,** archdeacon of Ecija. In Seville alone over 4000 Jews were murdered and their property, including synagogues, destroyed. The violence spread rapidly, and the juderías of Barcelona, Valencia, and Toledo, among many others, were virtually wiped out; few of them ever recovered to any extent. Those not slaughtered were compelled to accept baptism to save their skins, although some fled or remained unconverted. Perhaps as many as 200,000 Jews were thus forced to convert, at least ostensibly, and were known as *Conversos* or *New Christians.* They were as a matter of course regarded with considerable suspicion as false believers, secret judaizers, and practisers of Jewish rites —which many undoubtedly did— and were to become more distrusted than the Jews themselves, a veritable «fifth colum» within the body of the Catholic Church itself.

Prejudiced *Old* Christians continued to object to the prominent part they continued to play in Christian society, and so they continued to suffer social ostracism and anti-semitical smears and insinuations, which only exacerbated the already unstable situation.

In 1412 Queen **Catherine of Lancaster** pressed for the separation and confinement of Jews to special areas in towns of Castile, creating the *Barrio Nuevo* name that has survived in some places to our day. In 1412 the so-called *Laws of Valladolid* proposed by Bishop **Pablo de Santa María** (previously Salomon Halevi, chief rabbi of Burgos, who had opportunely converted in 1390) and the Valencian «saint» **Vicent Ferrer,** was an additional example of savage anti-semitic legislation. The following year the anti-Pope Benedict XIII (Papa Luna) convened the *Disputation of Tortosa,* at which Jews were arraigned and forced to debate with **Jerónimo de Santa Fe** (another convert, once named Joshua Halorki), and many were threatened with death if they did not accept baptism; and in its offensive way it was effective in greatly increasing the number of Conversos in Spain. The alarming growth of this potentially subversive element presented a serious challenge to the old aristocracy, for numerous conversos were now marrying into the Castilian and Aragonese nobility, and before long membership of the nobility was in itself suspicion of «unclean» blood. The highest ranks of the clergy were likewise contaminated. Numbers of prelates were conversos or of Jewish extraction, while both the first Inquisitors General —**Tomás de Torquemada** and **Diego de Deza,**— were of Jewish descent. It would be superfluous to cite further examples here.

While presumably a proportion of the New Christians were sincere in their conversion to Catholicism, many, if not most, continued to practise Jewish rites in secret, and little love was lost on the new faith imposed on them. Although no longer segregated, they were the butt of public resentment, particularly from the Old Christians, who formed an increasingly prominent part in both municipal and ecclesiastical administration, who disliked having to share power with men whom they considered of mixed blood and doubtful orthodoxy, and there were riots in Toledo in 1449 and again in 1467, which led to a statute excluding conversos from public office there. The former disturbances were sparked off by a heavy tax levied by the Crown, and the tax-farmer was a converso, who was as a matter of course accused of profiteering from local maladministration. Such calumnies were a commonplace, for they were particularly vulnerable, and it is by no means impossible that peculation did occasionally take place. At the time it was declared that «the so-called *Conversos*, offspring of perverse Jewish ancestors, must be held by law to be *infamous and ignominious, unfit and unworthy to hold any public office or benefice within the city of Toledo or hold lands within its jurisdiction,* or to be commissioners for oaths or notaries, or to have any authority over the true Christians of the Holy Catholic Church».

But, being Christians, or baptised as such, the conversos could not at first be barred from ecclesiastical, municipal, or royal offices on religious grounds; and soon —particularly in the mid 16C— the obsessive criterion for advancement became purity of blood *(limpieza de sangre),* an idea which in fact originally had Jewish connotations. A man had not only to prove that he was a faithful Catholic and not a convert, but also that his ancestors had likewise been Catholic —the issues were not now merely religious, but also social, economic, or even racial. Being of peasant stock became the best guarantee of unmixed blood and an asset to reach the highest Concils of the Realm. Purity of pedigree applied also for entry into the military orders, and the Colegios Mayores at the universities. Such diverse elements as pestilence, bad harvests, or price inflation, all of which effected the urban economy, were enough to provoke anti-semitic unrest, causing riots at Valladolid in 1470; in 1473 the conversos of Córdoba were expelled, and numerous minor massacres took place throughout conquered Andalucía in the 1470s.

The Catholic Kings had at first presented themselves as protectors of the Jews. Indeed, Isabella owed her throne and her marriage to Ferdinand largely to the support and counsel of Rabbi Abraham Senior of Segovia. In April 1481, however, they ordered them to be confined to their juderías. During the next decade unconverted Jews were expelled piecemeal from different dioceses throughout the country, among them, in 1487, those of conquered Andalucía. On 31 March, 1492, less than three months after they had entered Nasrid Granada in triumph (having in *Moorish* costume received the infidel's surrender) the Catholic Kings issued a general edict of expulsion. It is worth noting that Jewish financiers —among them Abraham Senior, who later converted— supplied very considerable funds for this last stage of the Christian reconquest. It has been estimated that between 150,000 and 400,000 Jews were forced to abandon Spain, where their ancestors had lived for over a thousand years: the number of those who remained cannot be estimated. Perhaps as many as 120,000 of the *Sephardim,* the majority from Castile, left for Portugal, whence they were in their turn partially expelled in 1497 or forcibly converted: others sailed to North Africa. They had to leave behind any gold, silver, or precious stones they owned, and their property was often sold for a song. Some made their way to England, Holland, Italy, Greece, and Morocco or crossed the frontier into France, many settling in the vicinity of Bayonne or Perpignan; others sought refuge as far away as Turkey (Salonica, Constantinople, Smyrna, Rhodes). Still another group of Christian-born Conversos found refuge in Spain's American Colonies. (See Bibliography). Many later returned discreetly to Spain, which supplemented the one-third to half of the Jewish-Converso community which remained in the country, accepting nominal baptism to a worse fate in a foreign field.

Meanwhile, since 1478/80, the Inquisition had been established in Spain by Papal decree not long after the queen's visit to Seville, where she had been profoundly influenced by the rabid preaching of **Alonso de Espi-**

na, in which he had reiterated the danger of harbouring false converts, for Isabel, the determined bigot that she was, remained entirely preoccupied with the extirpation of the pernicious errors of heresy from her realm, and saw little importance in the fact that commerce was on the decline. The disappearance of the Jews and the persecution of the Conversos had created a void in the world of capital which was never satisfactorily filled by the old Christians. Business slipped into the hands of foreign traders and capitalists, among them the Genoese, Italians, Germans, and Portuguese: Old Christian or Castilian financiers were in a minotiry.

And it was also in Seville, on 6 February 1481, that the first *auto de fé* was «celebrated», to use the contemporary term. It was to examine the genuinness of the conversion of Jews and Conversos who had remained in Spain and who had by now permeated the highest ranks of society that the Inquisition was established. The heretics brought to light here more than justified —in the minds of the Church and the Crown— the introduction of other «cleansing» tribunals throughout the country, While in the first eight years of life of the Seville tribunal alone, according to the contemporary chronicler **Andrés Bernáldez,** «more than 700 persons were burnt and over 5000 punished».

In 1482 Pope Sixtus IV issued a remarkable bull, probably at the request of wealthy Conversos, in which he categorically stated that the Inquisition had

> for some time been moved not by zeal for the faith and the salvation of souls, but by lust for wealth, and that many true and faithful Christians, on the testimony of enemies, rivals, slaves, and other lower and even less proper persons, have without any legitimate proof been thrust into secular prisons, tortured and condemned as relapsed heretics, deprived of their goods and property and handed over to the secular arm to be executed, to the peril of souls, setting a pernicious example, and causing disgust to many.

But any relic of papal authority had by now passed into the hands of the King of Aragón, Fernando, who, outraged by such interference, bitterly complained, and the bull was suspended. But for the long history of the «Holy Office», as the Inquisition was named, the reader is best advised to peruse Henry Kamen's balanced study *The Spanish Inquisition* (1965, although according to Luis Suárez Fernández, certain statements and conclusions are now outdated). The course of the Inquisition in Spanish America (established in Lima in 1570, and in Mexico City the following year, is beyond the scope of this Introduction; (see Bibliography).

It may be mentioned here that among eminent Spaniards of Jewish or Converso extraction during the 15-16Cs were the Valencian poet Ausias March; Hernando del Pulgar, the chronicler; the Humanist Juan Luis Vives; fray Luis de León; Saint Teresa of Avila; and the dramatist Fernando de Rojas.

In 1502, not satisfied with the rate of conversion, it was decreed that the Muslim population of the recently conquered Kingdom of Granada, as well as the Mudéjars of Castile, should also be expelled or converted (when they were known as *Moriscos);* and the order was extended to Aragón in 1525. In 1526 the Inquisition was established in Granada, where regulations with regard to the use of Arabic, of Moorish rites, customs, and clothes were enacted, but not stringently enforced until the edict of 1567.

Thus were sown the seeds of widespread disturbances throughout the following century, from the revolt of the *Comuneros* in Castile (1519-20), in which the cities were supported by disaffected nobles; in 1568 the Moriscos rebelling in the Alpujarras and the mountains of Granada, having appealed to the king of Fez for support, were only repressed with difficulty two years later. The decree for their actual expulsion was promulgated by Philip III in 1609, when some 275,000 of the estimated half a million (of a total population of about nine million Spaniards) left her shores, yet further impoverishing the country. It is now generally admitted that Spain has never entirely recovered from these various forced expulsions, a sad reflection on the intolerance of the Catholic Church in Spain in its endeavour to impose orthodoxy, and the rancorous spirit of the «honourable» Old Christians who supported it.

In 1526 the *Enchiridion* of Erasmus first appeared in Spanish translation, and had considerable influence, particularly among Conversos, and it was accordingly banned in 1559. In about 1545 the first official *Index of Forbidden Books* was drawn up in Spain, the first step in the Church's attempt to impose censorship of the written word and to prevent the entry of heretical doctrines into the country, where the sources of knowledge dried up and science ceased to exist, as **Feijóo** was later to lament. But the Jews, admittedly driven underground, still existed in Spain. Henry Swinburne, who visited the country in the 1770s, remarked that

> with a little discretion you may live here in what manner you please, but not if a Jew, who must on landing —he was describing Barcelona— declare himself to be such to the Inquisition, which immediately appoints a familiar to attend him all the time he stays ashore»; but he had been assured «that a Jew may travel from Perpignan to Lisbon, and sleep every night in the house of a Jew, being recommended from one to another; and that you may take it for granted, that wherever you see a house remarkably decked out with images, relics, and lamps, and the owner noted for being the most enthusiastic devotee of the parish, there it is ten to one but that the family are Israelites at heart.

But as late as 1802 **Carlos IV** decreed that no Israelite could enter Spain without leave being granted by the Inquisition, and it was only in 1834 that the long moribund «Holy Office» formally ceased to exist, and the property of the Church sequestered under the aegis of **Mendizábal**, himself of Jewish origin.

The Catholic Church in Spain was briefly brought back —in gratitude— to a position of power during the dictatorship of **Franco,** its political activists being largely responsible for fomenting the military rebellion against the Republican government in 1936. Franco's government looked unkindly on the influx of Ashkenazi Jews from central Europe and later from German-occupied Europe, although by the summer of 1942 some 20,000 refugees had passed through Spain, while another 5600 crossed the frontier during the second half of II World War. A few who had crossed the border illegally were sent back to France during the earlier period. Very few of them remained in Spain. Small communities grew, however, around those refugees and some Sephardim of North African extraction. Madrid and Barcelona were the first to be tolerated by Franco's fundamentalist approach to religious matters, thanks largely to a certain pressure brought to bear by the US government in the late 40's and 50's.

A communal centre and temple in Madrid was dedicated in 1968 when the edict of expulsion of 1492 was formally repealed.

It was not however until the proclamation of the new

Constitution of 1979 that all differential treatment before the law of Catholics and non-Catholics was officially suppressed.

A chapter of Bnai Brith has been active in Madrid for several years.

The *Asociación de Relaciones Culturales España-Israel (ARCEI)* was founded in Barcelona in 1978.

In 1982 an association named *Amistad España-Israel* was founded. A number of prominent personalities are to be counted among its members.

*

Present day Jewish population of Spain can be estimated at some 15,000 souls. A majority of its members are of Sephardic extraction, mostly from Morocco. There is an undetermined number of South American (Ashkenazi) families, very active in their professions, the liberal arts, and in communications, even if they are not very conspicuous in their participation in Jewish social life.

The standing population is marked by its origins and their peculiar adaptation to Spanish life. Predominant among their activities are business — trade and finance— and a few follow the professions of medicine, architecture, etc.

The leading communities are those of Madrid and Barcelona, both sharing equal parts of about two-thirds of the total national population. The remaining third is scattered among cities such as like Valencia, Málaga, Seville, and also the Canary Islands, and the two Spanish enclaves on the Moroccan coast —Ceuta and Melilla, whence many families originated—

The communities are independent but are loosely linked by the Federación de Comunidades Israelitas de España. As a rule all services adhere to the Sephardic rite. In the leading communities, however, it is possible to attend Ashkenazi services on certain occasions.

Kosher food is available only at some communal centres and it is advisable to check with them in advance.

For a list of Jewish communities in contemporary Spain, see p. 115.

BIBLIOGRAPHY

Grouped below are a selected number of comparatively recently published books on Spain and the Jews in Spain, which may be found useful or of interest to the average traveller, and will themselves contain bibliographies for further or more specialised reading. Many are in English; some are tendentious. Not all are specifically concerned with the Sephardic Jews, but will describe their position in an historical context.

They have been put into two main groups: A, those concerning the Jews in Spain before 1492; and B, after that date. In certain cases there is an overlap.

The main bibliography of the subject is R. Singerman, *The Jews in Spain and Portugal; a Bibliography* (1975), while much information will also be found in *The Encyclopedia Judaica* (16 volumes; 1971), and the bi-annual periodical *Sefarad* (Revista del Instituto de Estudios Hebraicos, Sefardíes y de Oriente Próximo), published from 1941 in Spanish by the Instituto Arias Montano, Medinaceli 4, Madrid 14. They also publish a number of monographs, etc.

A JEWISH HISTORY: Yitzhak Baer, *A History of the Jews in Christian Spain* (1966), largely based on his *Die Juden in Christlischen Spanien* (reprinted 1969, with an additional bibliography by Haim Beinart); the 1981 Spanish edition (Altalena) contains updated bibliographical information; Abraham A. Neuman, *The Jews in Spain* (1948; reprinted 1969); Eliyahu Astor, *The Jews in Moslem Spain* (1973; 1979); S. Katz, *The Jews in Visigothic and Frankish Kingdoms of Spain and Gaul* (1937; reprinted 1970); Américo Castro, *The Spaniards* (1971), the previous edition of which was entitled *The Structure of Spanish History* (1954), being an adaptation of his *España en su historia: Cristianos, moros y judíos* (1948); L. García Iglesias, *Los Judíos en la España antigua* (1978); Luis Suárez Fernández, *Judíos españoles en la Edad Media* (1980), and *Documentos acerca de la Expulsión de los judíos* (1964); J. Amador de los Ríos, *Historia de los Judíos de España* (1875; reprinted 1973), *Estudios históricos, políticos y literarios sobre los judíos de España* (1848; reprinted 1942), and with Fidel Fita, *La España hebrea* (1889-90); M. Kriegel, *Les juifs à la fin de Moyen Ages dans l'Europe méditerranéenne* (1979); J. M. Lacalle, *Los judíos españoles* (1961); Frederick David Mocatta, *The Jews of Spain and Por-*

tugal and the Inquisition (1877; reprinted 1973); Haim Avni, *Spain, the Jews and Franco* (1982).

GENERAL HISTORY: E. A. Thompson, *The Goths in Spain* (1969); Gabriel Jackson, *The Making of Medieval Spain* (1972); Angus Mackay, *Spain in the Middle Ages* (1977); W. Montgomery Watt, *A History of Islamic Spain* (1965); J. N. Hillgarth, *The Spanish Kingdoms, 1250-1516* (1976; 1978); Joseph F. O'Callaghan, *A History of Medieval Spain* (1975); Jaime Vicens Vives, *An Economic History of Spain* (1969); Thomas F. Glick, *Islamic and Christian Spain in the Early Middle Ages* (1979); S. D. F. Goitein, *Letters of Medieval Jewish Traders* (1973), and *A Mediterranean Society* (1967); Harold Livermore, *The Origins of Spain and Portugal* (1971); M. P. Hornik (ed.), *Collected Studies in honour of Américo Castro's Eightieth Year* (1965); J. H. Elliott, *Imperial Spain, 1469-1716* (1963).

LOCAL HISTORY: Justiniano Rodríguez Fernández, *La Judería de la ciudad de León* (1969), and *Juderías de la Provincia de León* (1976); Pilar León Tello, *Judíos de Avila* (1963), and *Judíos de Toledo* (1979); A Carlos Merchán Fernández, *Los judíos de Valladolid* (1976); Baruch Braunstein, *The Chuetas of Majorca* (1936; reprinted 1972); Lucien Wolf, *Jews in the Canary Islands* (1926); Abraham Lionel Isaacs, *The Jews of Majorca* (1936); Antonio Pons, *Los judíos del Reino de Mallorca durante los siglos XIII y XIV* (1958).

ART AND CULTURE: Francisco Cantera Burgos, *Sinagogas españolas* (1955), reprinted 1984; J. M. Millás Vallicrosa, *Las inscripciones hebraicas de España* (1956).

B THE SEPHARDIM. *In general:* R. D. Barnett (ed.), *The Sephardi Heritage* (Vol. 1, 1971); Julio Caro Baroja, *Los judíos en la España moderna y contemporánea* (1st ed. in 3 vols, 1962; 2nd ed. 1978); M. J. Benardete, *Hispanic Culture and Character of the Sephardic Jews in the Near East* (1953); Albert M. Hyamson, *The Sephardim of England* (1952); Seymour B. Liebman, *The Jews in New Spain* (1970), *Requiem for the Forgotten. The Jews in New Spain 1493-1815* (1982); Federico Ysart, *España y los judíos en la Segunda Guerra Mundial* (1973); Haim Avni, *Spain, the Jews and Franco* (1982).

CONVERSOS: Josep M. Solà-Solé, Samuel G. Armistead, and Joseph H. Silverman, *Hispania Judaica* (1980); Albert A. Sicroff, *Les controverses des statuts de «Pureté de Sang» en Espagne du XV au XVII siècle* (1960); Américo Castro, *De la Edad Conflictiva* (1961); Antonio Domínguez Ortiz, *La clase social de los conversos en Castilla en la Edad Moderna* (1955), and *Los conversos de origen judío después de la Expulsión* (1957); Marcel Bataillon, *Erasme et l'Espagne* (1937; trans. into Spanish 1950).

MARRANOS: Benzion Netanyahu, *The Marranos of Spain,*

from the late XIVth to the early XVI Century (1966; reprinted 1973); Cecil Roth, *A History of the Marranos* (1932; 4th ed. 1974); Yosef Haim Yerushalmi, *From Spanish Court to Italian Ghetto — Isaac Cardoso: a Study in 17C Marranism and Jewish Apologetics* (1971); Lucien Wolf, *Report on the «Marranos» or Crypto-Jews of Portugal* (1926); Julio Caro Baroja, *Razas, pueblos y linajes* (1957); J. Lúcio de Azevedo, *História dos Cristãos Novos Portugueses* (1921; reprinted 1975).

INQUISITION: Charles Henry Lea, *A History of the Inquisition in Spain* (1906-8; reprinted 1966), *The Moriscos of Spain* (1901; reprinted 1980) and *History of the Inquisition in the Spanish Dependencies* (1908; reprinted 1922?); J. Llorente, *A Critical History of the Inquisition* (1823 ed.; reprinted 1967), being a translation of his *Historia crítica de la Inquisición de España* (various editions since 1818/23); Louis Cardillac, *Morisques et Chrétiens* (1977); Ricardo García Cárcel, *Orígenes de la Inquisición española: el tribunal de Valencia, 1478-1530* (1976); Cecil Roth, *The Spanish Inquisition* (1937); Henry Kamen, *The Spanish Inquisition* (1965); Alexandre Herculano, *History of the Origin and Establishment of the Inquisition in Portugal* (reprint of the English translation; 1972); Julio Caro Baroja, *Inquisición, Brujería y Criptojudaísmo* (1970), *El Señor Inquisidor y otras vidas por oficio* (1968), and *Los moriscos del reino de Granada*; N. López Martínez, *Los judaizantes castellanos y la Inquisición en tiempo de Isabel la Católica* (1954); Boleslao Lewin, *La Inquisición en Hispanoamérica* (1962); Bartolomé Bennassar, *L'Inquisition espagnole: XVᵉ-XIXᵉ siècle* (1979); Haim Beinart, *Records of the Trials of the Spanish Inquisition in Ciudad Real* (1974); Antonio José Saraiva, *Inquisição e cristãos-novos* (1969), and *A Inquisição Portuguesa* (1956); Antonio Márquez, *Literatura e Inquisición en España, 1478-1834* (1980); Marcelin Defourneaux, *Inquisición y censura de libros en la España del siglo XVIII* (1973).

GLOSSARY

Aggadah   Parts of the *Talmud* and *Midrash* containing homiletic expositions of the Bible, etc. as distinct from the *Halakhah,* concerned with rabbinic law; narrative of the Exodus read in Pesah.

Aljama   Name to designate the Jewish community living in a Christian town; sometimes used synonimously for *Judería.*

Ashkenazim   General denomination of Jews from Central and Eastern Europe.

Auto-de-fe (or da-fé)   Literally an «act of Faith», the ceremony at which penitent heretics were publicly «reconciled» to the Catholic Church. The actual execution usually by burning of convicted heretics was entrusted to the secular arm, and did not form part of the proceedings.

Av bet din   Head of a *bet din* or rabbinical court of law.

Bet ha-midrash   A school for higher rabbinic studies, often attached to a synagogue.

Call   In Aragón, the word used to designate the *aljama* (see above).

Chueta   Term applied to Majorcan families of Jewish ancestry.

Converso   Term applied to Christianised Moors and Jews and their descendants; also known as «New Christians».

Crypto-Jew   Term applied to Jew ostensibly observing Christianity, but remaining at heart a Jew, and maintaining Jewish observances in secret: see *Marrano.*

Diáspora   A reference to the dispersion of the Jews; a Jew living outside Israel.

Familiar   A lay associate of the Holy Office responsible for informing on acts or words that might constitute heresy.

Hanukkah   8-day celebration commemorating Judah Maccabee's victory over Antiochus Epiphanes, the Syrian, and subsequent re-dedication of the Temple (4C BCE).

Hanukkiya   Nine-candle holder used in Hanukka festivities.

Herem   Excommunication imposed by rabbinical authorities for a breach of discipline, religious or communal.

Hermandad   A peace-keeping brotherhood organised as a police force in the 15C.

Holy Office   Synonym for the *Inquisition*.

Inquisition   Tribunal of the Catholic Church responsible for maintaining the purity of the faith.

Judería   The sector of a town inhabited by Jews: see *aljama*.

Kabbalah   The Jewish mystical tradition.

Karaites   A segment of Jewish tradition whose adherents rejected all rabbinical laws —and Talmud—, only accepting the Written Law of the *Torah*.

Kasher; also *Kosher*   Ritually pure food.

Ketubbah   Marriage contract.

Ladino   Dialect of Castilian, used as an everyday language by the Sephardim.

Libro Verde de Aragón   Literally a «green book», applied to genealogical studies tracing the Jewish ancestry of the nobility after the 16C.

Limpieza de sangre   Literally «purity of blood», a term referring to the ensemble of regulations and measures adopted from mid-15C onward aiming at excluding Spaniards of Jewish descent from public office, armed forces, the Church, and other employing bodies.

Marrano   Term to designate an ostensibly Christianised Jew, who remained Jewish in private; a term likewise applied to their descendants, who usually reverted publicly to Judaism when away from Spain. In Hebrew *anusim*.

Menorah   Seven-branched candlestick.

Morisco   A Christianised Moslem remaining in reconquered Spain after 1492; or a Moor nominally baptised.

Mozárabe   Term denoting a Christian living under Moorish rule.

Mudéjar   A Moslem living in Christian Spain; a term usually applied to their decoration and architecture.

Muwallad or **Muladí**   A Christian converted to Islam.

New Christian synonym for a *Converso*.

Pesah   Passover festival commemorating the Jewish exodus from Egypt.

Purim   Festival held to commemorate the delivery of the Jews of Persia in the time of Esther (6C BCE).

Rosh Ha-Shanah   Two-day holiday traditionally marking the New Year.

Sanbenito   A penitential garment prescribed by the Inquisition (a corruption of *saco bendito*).

Sephardim   General denomination of Jews, mostly from Spain and Portugal (but also from the South of France and parts of Italy) and their descendants, wherever resident, as distinct from *Ashkenazim*.

Sefer Torah   Manuscript scroll of the *Torah*.

Shema   Judaism's confession of faith, proclaiming the absolute unity of God (Deut. 6:4) (Shemá-Israel Adonai Elohenu Adonai Ehad).

Sukkot   Festivals of Tabernacles.

Takkanah   Regulations governing the internal life of communities and congregations supplementing the Law of the Torah.

Talmud   A compendium of «teaching» or discussions on the *Mishnah* (the earliest codification of Jewish oral law) by generations of scholars and jurists over a period of several centuries.

Torah   The first five books of the Bible.

Yom Kippur   Day of Atonement, a solemn fast.

Zohar   Mystical commentary on the Pentateuch; the main textbook of *Kabbalah*.

TOWNS
(A - Z)

Topographical Introduction

The Jewish communities in medieval Spain were distributed very widely; almost every port or town of any consequence contained a small community, but in a very large number of cases this is known merely through some passing reference in tax returns, etc. Numerous assumptions have been made as to the probability of Jews having at one time resided in certain places; but they may just as well have been in many other towns or villages of which there is no written record of a Jewish community; or at least research has not yet uncovered some confirmatory reference. Claims have been made that Jews existed in a number of minor sites not included in this Guide, in which an attempt has been made to cite all those places in which remains of Jewish interest may *still* be seen; while in an appendix a number of places of secondary interest have been described, even if there is no longer anything to see there to remind one of a Jewish community in the past.

On the Spanish mainland —although Ceuta, on the North African coast; and Palma de Mallorca in the Balearics are also listed— the main places of interest are to be found in the following areas: A, *Catalonia* and the *Valencian coast;* B, a few specific towns in *Andalucía;* C, *Extremadura;* D, *Aragón* and *Navarre;* E, the *Castiles* and *León.*

Listed below are a few itineraries which may be followed, which take in the majority of the more important towns listed.

A   Entering Spain from France (Perpignan), we may make the short detour from Figueras to *Besalú,* regaining the main road at *Girona,* and thence follow the motorway to *Barcelona. Vic* lies

La Coruña

Valmaseda

M. de Ebr

Ribadavia

Aguilar de Campoo   Oña
León   Cea   Herrera   Briviesca   Har
Astorga   C. de los Condes   Burgos   Ná
Orense   Sahagún   Castrojeriz

Palencia

Dueñas

Zamora   Valladolid   Berlan

Medina del Campo

Sepúlveda   Sig

Salamanca   Arévalo   Coca
Alba de Tormes   Segovia   Med

Ciudad Rodrigo   Avila   Alcalá de Henares
Béjar   Madrid
Hervás   Maqueda   Illescas   H
Plasencia   Toledo
Alcántara   Talavera de la Reina
Cáceres   Trujillo   Guadalupe

Badajoz   Ciudad Real
Almagro

Llerena

Córdoba
Jaén
Ecija   Lucena
Carmona   Sevilla   Alcalá de Guadaira   Elvira   Gr

Jerez de la Frontera   Ad

Málaga
Cádiz
Gibraltar
Ceuta

Jaca

Besalú

Huesca　Barbastro　　　　　　　Girona

Tudela　　　　　Monzón　Balaguer　　Vic

Alagón　A. de Cinca　　　　Agramunt

Zaragoza　　　　　Lleida　Cervera

　　　　　Fraga　　Tárrega　　　Barcelona

Santa Coloma de Queralt

aroca　　　V. del Penedés　　Tarragona

　　　　　　Tortosa

Alcañiz

Morella

Albarracín

Teruel　Segorbe

uenca　　　　　Castellón
　　　　　　de la Plana

Burriana　　　　　　Palma de Mallorca

Murviedro

Valencia

Játiva

Elche

Orihuela

Murcia

Cartagena

some 66 km N of the later. From Barcelona we may follow the motorway to *Tarragona*, which later by-passes *Tortosa*. We continue S via *Sagunto* to *Valencia*, some 60 km S of which lies *Xativa*. From Valencia may turn NW via *Teruel* to *Daroca*, and *Calatayud* (see D).

B   A circuit of the main towns of Andalucía of Jewish interest may be made with ease from *Córdoba* to *Granada*, and thence to *Málaga*. From Málaga we may bear NW via Osuna to *Seville*, and then return via *Carmona* and Ecija to Córdoba. *Lucena* lies 73 km S of the latter.

C   *Toledo* is probably best visited from *Madrid;* *Maqueda* lies 42 km N E of the former, which is also by-passed on the road from Madrid to *Talavera*, and *Trujillo* (on the road W via Mérida and Badajoz to Lisbon). From Trujillo we may continue due W to *Cáceres* (NW of which lies *Alcántara)*, and thence N via *Plasencia* , *Hervás*, and *Béjar*, to *Salamanca*. We may return to Madrid via *Avila*, or continue N to Zamora (see E).

D   From Madrid we may drive NE via *Guadalajara*, *Sigüenza*, and *Medinaceli*, to *Calatayud*, some 40 km SE of which lies *Daroca*, thence continuing NE to *Zaragoza*. From *Lleida* to the E, we may swing NW via *Monzón* and *Barbastro* to *Huesca*, and thence via *Jaca* to *Pamplona*, before returning SW via *Estella*, and then S via *Calahorra* to *Tudela, Tarazona, Agreda, Soria, Almazán*, and *Atienza*.

E   From Madrid we may drive NE via *Segovia* to Valladolid, and thence to *Palencia*, and *Burgos*. From the latter we may either bear NE via Pancorbo and *Miranda de Ebro* to *Vitoria*; or alternatively W via Osorno (46 km N of which lies *Aguilar de Campóo), Carrión de los Condes*, and *Sahagún*, to *León*. From León continue W to *Astorga*, and the SE via Benavente to *Zamora* (65 km S of which lies Salamanca (see C above). From Zamora, we may return to Madrid via *Toro*, Tordesillas, Medina del Campo, and Arévalo.

In the entries for the most important towns we have included a schematic plan showing the approximate location of the points of interest.

For smaller places, we would recommend a brief stop at the local square and either asking for directions or trying to find the place by yourself. Both experiences may turn out to be most enjoyable.

*

Agramunt (4,300 inhab; 15 km N of Tárrega, prov. of Lleida-Lérida) had a small Jewish community in the 13C, and another 40 families settled there in 1316.

A tombstone with a Hebrew inscription is preserved in the *Ateneo* of Agramunt.

Agreda (3,600 inhab; 18km W of Tarazona, and 50 E of Soria) had a Judería on the S bank of the river Queiles opposite the Christian quarter, while above to the E stood the Morería on the flank of the hill dominated by the ruined castle «de la Muelas». On the SW side of the Judería stands the picturesque *Torre de los Castejones;* while on the N side of this district may have stood the synagogue, although the exact site is not known with any certainty.

Aguilar de Campóo (5,200 inhab; 25km N of Herrera de Pisuerga, prov. of Palencia, on the Santander road). This small fortified town had a settlement of Jews as early as 1187, but its Judería and synagogue were destroyed during the civil wars of the late 14C (some scholars believed it was sacked by the Black Prince troops), and their location is unknown.

On the *Puerta de Reinosa* is an inscription in Spanish, Hebrew, and Ladino (rare in Spain) confirming that it was constructed in 1380 by Don Çaq (Isaac), son of Solomon ibn Malak.

Alcalá de Henares (100,600 inhab; 31km E of Madrid), famous for its university founded in 1508, and the birthplace of Cervantes (1547-1616), author of *Don Quixote*, was captured from the Moors in 1118, when the Jews were granted numerous rights equal to the Christians.

The Marrano poet *Pero Ferrus* suggests that many members of its Converso community were tried by the Inquisition for continuing to visit the city's synagogues. *Cardinal Cisneros* encouraged the study of Hebrew, and it was here that in 1514-17 the great *Complutensian Polyglot Bible* was published (in Latin, Greek, Hebrew, and with parts in Chaldean). The Hebrew scholars were *Alfonso de Zamora, Alfonso de Alcalá*, and *Pablo Coronel*. It was superseded some 50 years later by the *Antwerp Polyglot Bible* prepared by *Benito Arias Montano*.

Alcántara (2,500 inhab; 62km N E of Cáceres, near the famous Roman Bridge). The hermitage known as the *Ermita de la Soledad* contains an inscription in Hebrew referring to the fact that it was constructed in 1335 by a certain *Mosé Lerma*, and it is possible that it was once a synagogue, for it is almost certain that a Jewish community existed here at what was then an important crossing of the river Tagus.

Astorga (12,200 inhab; 47km W of León) had a community in the 11C, protected by *fueros* or charters. They lived at first within the fortifications, but the Judería was later extended to an area around the *Calle de las Tiendas*. The *Paseo de la Sinagoga*, behind the Cathedral and Gaudí's Episcopal Palace, ran along the city walls. Many Jews were forcibly converted in 1230-31; others were persecuted in 1412, as were their co-religionists in León. They were strong enough to claim certain privileges exempting them from the payment of crown taxes in 1432 at the Synod of Valladolid; but 60 years later they were expelled.

Avila (33,500 inhab; capital of its province). A community referred to in 1085 had probably long existed there, which by 1303 numbered c.50

families. In 1366 they were attacked, and in 1375 forced to attend religious disputations between the apostate *Juan de Valladolid* and *Moses ha Kohn* of Tordesillas. In the late 15C the community was heavily taxed, and a number of restrictive measures imposed on them, and they were segregated to separate areas of the town.

In 1490 an inquisitorial tribunal was set up there, which claimed c.100 victims within the following decade. Their two synagogues were sold.

The main Judería lay near the *Puerta de San Vicente* (within the N E corner of the walled enceinte), around the *Capilla de Mosén Rubi,* and to-

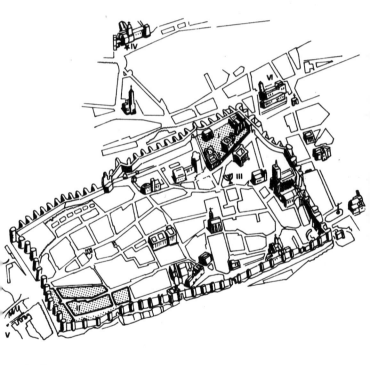

Avila
I. *Old Jewry.*
II. *New Jewry.*
III. *Probable location of main synagogue.*
IV. *Convent of la Encarnación, probably on an old Jewish cemetery.*
V. *Bears Enclosure, possibly on a new Jewish cemetery.*
VI. *Church of San Vicente.*

wards the *Puerta del Mariscal*. A Gothic doorway in the *Calle del Lomo* (at present called *de Esteban Domingo)* just N of the central covered market, may have been the entrance to the Synagogue. The *new* Judería lay within the SW corner of the walls, beyond which, to the SW of the bridge over the river Adaja, possibly lay its cemetery.

Another Jewish cemetery may have been sited near the Carmelite convent of *La Encarnación,* not far N of the town walls, where *Teresa de Cepeda y Ahumada* (1515-82) of Jewish lineage, took the veil in 1533, later being known as *Santa Teresa de Avila,* the town's most famous native.

The burial-place of the notorious Inquisitor-General *Tomás de Torquemada* (1420-98) is the Sacristy of the *Convent of Santo Tomás,* some distance SE of the walls.

Barbastro (12,900 inhab; 52km SE of Huesca). In 1144 *Count Ramón Berenguer IV* conferred an estate on *Zecri,* a Jew of Barbastro, in reward for his services; while in 1179 *Benjamin Abenbitals* and *Joseph ben Solomon* were granted permission by the Bishop de Huesca to erect shops near the cathedral, probably a converted mosque, and not rebuilt until the early 16C.

The main Jewish quarter from the mid 13C was the citadel, where they were subjected to siege in 1391. The community ceased to exist in the first quarter of the 15C, although it became a Converso centre, and its synagogue was converted into a church.

Barcelona (1,751,100 inhab, excluding adjacent municipalities; the capital of Cataluña). One of the oldest Jewish communities in the peninsula, referred to in the 9C, while an Arab chronicler stated that there were as many Jews as Christians in the city: only 60 Jewish names appear in a list of 1079, however.

From this period the Judería lay in the heart of the old city, near the port, and was traversed by the *Calle del Call* (Kahal), leading SW from the *Plaza Sant Jaume*. At the S end of the parallel *Ca-*

lle Marlet (a lane just to the W), at its junction with the *Arco de San Ramón del Call,* a Jewish lapidary inscription has been set into the wall, below which is a Spanish translation. It reads: «Hekdesh (a gift donated in charity) of Rabbi Samuel Hasardi may his soul rest in peace». The wall adjacent to No 5 in the street was probably that of the Judería. Further S, to the SE of the junction of the Calle del Call with the *Calle Banys Nous,* stood the *Jewish Baths,* which were destroyed in 1834. A maquette may be seen in the *Museo de Historia de la Ciudad,* which is of very considerable interest in itself. Almost opposite this point, on the W side of the adjacent *Calle de Fernando* (or *Ferran*) stands the Gothic church of *Sant Jaume,* erected in 1393 on the site of a synagogue.

Barcelona

1. *Plaza Calvo Sotelo.*
2. *Avenida Diagonal.*
3. *Calle del Porvenir. (Synagogue)*
4. *Travesía de Gracia.*
5. *Calle Montaner*

Their principal cemetery stood on the hill of Montjuic (Mons Judaicus) overlooking the harbour, where a number of tombstones have been found, which are preserved in the *Archaeological Museum*, and in the castle of Montjuic.

In 1263 took place an organised religious dispute known as the *Disputation of Barcelona*, between *Nahmanides* and Christian ecclesiastics including *Raymond de Peñafort* but the sessions, over which *King Jaime I of Aragón* presided, were interrupted at an early stage. The Jewish community were largely employed as artisans and merchants, while some were engaged in the mint: coins bearing the names of Jewish goldsmiths date back to the first half of the 11C.

The Jews of Barcelona flourished in the 13C, in 1306 being augmented by some 60 co-religionists from France, but the jealousy of Christian merchants caused the king to restrict the activities of Jewish traders with Syria and Egypt; while the Judería was also attacked during the plague of 1348. In c.1367 it was claimed that the Jews had desecrated the Host, and several Jews were killed and their leaders briefly imprisoned. Far more serious was the rioting of 1391, in spite of protection offered by the city fathers, when, instigated by a band of Castilians who had arrived by sea, the Judería was sacked. Within the week some 400 Jews were killed: the rest were ostensibly converted, to save their skins. Some rioters were condemned to the gallows, but the majority were acquitted. Although *King Jaime I* endeavoured to rehabilitate the community, allotting them a new residential quarter and restoring their former privileges and (temporary) tax exemption, few were prepared to take advantage of the offer, and within the decade *King Martin*, under further pressure from the burghers, finally prohibited their re-establishment.

Meanwhile renewed prosperity was brought to Barcelona by the commercial acumen and activity of the Conversos, until in 1486 —in the face of protest by the city fathers— *Fernando of Aragón* introduced the Inquisition to Barcelona. While problems of procedure were being discussed, many of the more prominent merchants fled, taking with them their portable capital: credit and commerce rapidly declined. A number of important officials of Converso descent were subsequently charged with observing Jewish rites, and were put to death.

Some 400 years later, at the beginning of the present century, a number of Jews from as far afield as Turkey and the Balkans, most of them of Spanish origin, resettled in Barcelona, encouraged by the Spanish government. From 1918, when there were about 100 Jews in the city, the number rose to over 3000 in 1932, and over 5000 by 1935, the Sephardim then in the minority. Some found it convenient to leave the city at the end of the Civil War, most of them moving to France or Palestine. In 1984 the community numbered c.4000, both Sephardi and Ashkenazi.

Béjar (17,300 inhab; 72 km S of Salamanca), an important wool market, undoubtedly had a Jewish community, but all that remains is the door of a *Synagogue* in the *Calle de 29 de Agosto* (numbers 3, 5, and 7), near the *Palace of the Dukes* and the *Iglesia de la Antigua*. In the entrance of the palace is a replica of the so-called «Lápida de doña Fadueña», with its Hebrew inscription, the original of which is to be seen in the Museo Sefardí, Toledo.

Berlanga de Duero (1900 inhab; 25km SE of El Burgo de Osma, province of Soria) retains a district still known as *La Yubería* (sic), extending between the *Mirador de las Monjas* and the street known as *«de Jeraiz»*.

Besalú (2000 inhab; 34 km NW of Girona) was one of the oldest communities in Cataluña, with its Judería huddled close to the Romanesque *Bridge,* which here spans the river Fluviá, and which was threaded by the *Calle del Pont* as far as the *Plaza Mayor.* The earliest tombstone with a Hebrew inscription found there is dated 1090. Although they were defended by the king against

Dominican interference in 1292, they were attacked during the Easter riots of 1331. They were again protected by the local authorities during the pogrom of 1391, but were nevertheless included in the general expulsion of 1492.

The main extant relic of their long residence there is the *Jewish Bath* or *mikve*, discovered by chance as recently as 1964, which may be visited. They lie close to the bridgehead, and are approached by a passage and 36 steps. The paved bath-room itself, some 4.50 m by 5.50 m, with a vaulted roof, and which may be entered with ease, isone of the more interesting relics of the Jewish heritage remaining in Spain apart from the more obvious and famous synagogues still extant.

Burgos (132,900 inhab; capital of its province), an important centre of trade, had a Jewish community in the 11C, and settlements in the vicinity date from 974. By the end of the 13C it had become the largest Jewish community in Old Castile, with some 150 families resident there.

It was here that the *Cid* imposed on Jewish money-lenders by leaving them an iron-bound chest filled with sand rather than gold as a surety for a loan to finance his campaigns; but he later honestly redeemed his pledge. The actual «cofre del Cid» —according to tradition— may be seen in the Cloister of the *Cathedral*.

Enrique de Trastámara extracted a large sum from the Burgos Jewry, and declared a moratorium on Jewish loans to Christians. Later, in 1379, Jewish trading outside the Judería was prohibited. After the pogrom of 1391 a number of Jews were ostensibly converted and settled in a special Converso quarter called the *Barriada de San Esteban*. During the next century the majority of those who remained gradually became amalgamated with the Christians. Among them was the Converso bishop, *Pablo de Santa María* (c.1350-1435), known prior to his baptism in 1390 as *Salomon Halevi*. He became bishop of Burgos in 1415, having previously been its chief rabbi.

The lower Judería (de Abajo) lay to the NW of

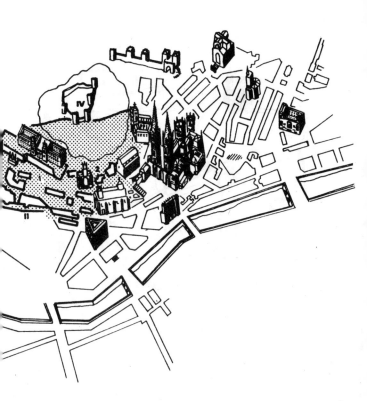

Burgos

I.   Church of San Esteban.
II.   Los Cubos (The towers).
III.   Old San Martín Gate.
IV.   Castle.
1.   Upper Jewry.
2.   Lower Jewry.

the *Cathedral* (founded 1221) on the lower slopes of the castle hill; while the upper Judería (de Arriba) extended further to the W and N of a remaining stretch of wall ending at the old *Puerta de San Martín*.

Cáceres (66,000 inhab; capital of its province). The old Jewish quarter was sited on a steep slope within the E wall of medieval Cáceres, bounded on the N by the *Arco del Cristo*, and by the *Casa de las Veletas* on the SW corner. It is threaded by the *Calle de San Antonio*, in which stands the *Ermita de San Antonio*, erected on the site of the former synagogue.

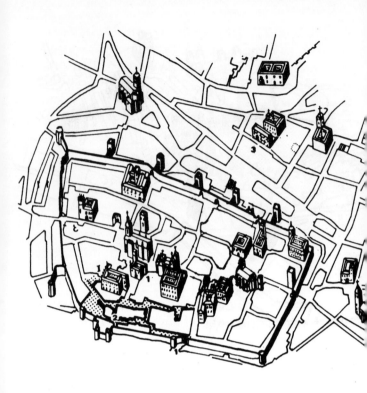

Cáceres
I.   *Casa de las Veletas*
1.   *Arco del Cristo*
2.   *Ermita de San Antonio*
3.   *Calle de la Cruz*

The *Calle de la Cruz*, parallel to, and W of *Plaza Mayor*, was probably the centre of a new judería, which later became that of the Converso population.

Calahorra (16,400 inhab; 49 km SE of Logroño). The community here is referred to in the mid-12C. By the 13C there were some 50 Jewish families resident here, but by 1370 a number left for Navarre, and the situation of those remaining deteriorated.

In August 1492 the synagogue was converted into a church, on the ruins of which the later church of *San Francisco* was erected; while settlers in what was the Judería were granted provisional exemptions from taxes. Nearby is *Calle de la Sinagoga*.

Calatayud (17,200 inhab; 87 km SW of Zaragoza) had a flourishing Jewish community during the Middle Ages, the earliest record of their presence there being a tombstone dated 919. In the mid 11C their number was estimated at 800, and the 300 Jewish families still there in 1391 were apparently not harmed during the anti-semitic disorders of that year, although after 1398 they were prohibited from residing without the Judería, which lay between the *Colegiata de Santa María la Mayor* and the W walls of the town. They also inhabited part of the fortress area.

They were represented at the *Disputation of Tortosa* in 1413-14 by *Samuel Halevi* and *Moses ben Musa*. Among its distinguished Conversos was *Yucef Abencabra,* who after his conversion took the name *Martín de la Cabra,* and in 1415 was responsible for converting one of the town's nine synagogues into a church.

Certain Jews were apparently dispossessed of their homes at this time, and threatened by the municipal authorities, but were later allowed to return, having complained to the king and on receiving his protection. Many of its Conversos are said to have reverted to Judaism, and the Inquisition remained active here between 1488 and 1502, a decade after its community had been expelled.

Antoinette de Loppes (López), Montaigne's mother, was descended from the Pazagon family, once prominent in the Judería of Calatayud.

Carmona (21,950 inhab; 33 km E of Seville) once contained a Judería, situated near the S wall of the town, which flourished during the 11C, but it suffered severely in the anti-semitic riots of 1391 and four years later its synagogue was destroyed. It is assumed, owing to the proximity of the *Calle de la Judería,* that the present church of *San Blas* was erected on its site.

Carrión de los Condes (2800 inhab; 52 km N of Palencia). A community was already resident there in 1225, its privileges serving as a model for the community at nearby Sahagún.

Shem Tov Ardutiel, otherwise known as *Santob of Carrión* (c.1290-c.1369), compiler of «Proverbios morales», was rabbi here in the mid 13C. Its fortunes revived after the pogrom of 1391; and many of its Jews were engaged in tax-farming activities. It is assumed that the Judería stood adjacent to the 12C church of *Santiago,* with its remarkable carved frieze, close to the *Plaza de Belén.*

Cervera (6200 inhab; 56 km E of Lleida). In c.1300 the Judería, containing some 30-40 families, lay between the *Call de Vent* and the *Call de Agramuntell;* it had its own cemetery. From 1369 the Jews — among them some physicians of repute— were restricted to this quarter, but as some members of the community resided without the walls, two synagogues were built. They survived various anti-semitic riots, and still owned considerable property in the mid 15C.

Ceuta (on the African coast opposite Gibraltar), an important harbour at the W end of the Mediterranean, had a Jewish community which during the Middle Ages was one of the most cultured and powerful in North Africa, until in 1148 it was persecuted by the Almohades.

It was in the 16C a refuge for Marranos and Jews exiled from Spain, but in 1580 it became a Spanish possession.

Its Jewish community was re-established in 1869; by 1969 it numbered some 600.

Ciudad Real (45,000 inhab; capital of its province), previously *Villa Real,* had a Jewish quarter on the E side of the town in the late 13C, which was destroyed in 1391. The specifically Jewish community was replaced by Conversos, who in 1449 —and sporadically during the following 25 years— were likewise persecuted. For two years, from 1483, a tribunal of the Inquisition was established there, and a number of Conversos —or ostensibly such— were burned at autos-de-fé.

The ancient Judería was situated within the

triangle flanked to the N by the *Calle de Calatra-va;* to the S by the *Calle de la Mata* (the latter being an extension of the main road entering the town from Daimiel).

Ciudad Rodrigo (13,000 inhab; 89 km S of Salamanca). Little is known of the community here, which was referred to in the 13C, but it was apparently flourishing in the 15C, before the town became a transit station of Jews leaving Spain for Portugal after 1492. In the same year the synagogue was converted into a church.

Córdoba (250,900 inhab; capital of its province), once the magnificent capital of the Omayyad caliphate, is said to have been handed over to the Moors by its disaffected Jewish inhabitants in 711, but the first reliable source referring to Jews in Córdoba is dated 840. In the following century the physician *Hasdai ibn Shaprut* attracted a number of Hebrew scholars and poets to the court of *Abderrahman III.* It was also the birthplace of *Moses ben Maimon* Maimonides (1135-1204), the influential rationalist rabbi, who left the city during the Almohad invasion, when its Jews were compelled to accept Islam. A statue to his memory was erected in 1964 not far S of the Synagogue in the small plaza of Tiberiades named after his presumed final resting place.

The earliest Jewish quarter lay to the SW of the city, near the *Alcázar,* and later extensions reached as far N as the church of *San Juan,* and —to the NE— the church of *Santa Clara,* and surrounding the *Mezquita* or mosque. Another Judería stood near the *Bab al-Yahud* (later the *Almodóvar Gate),* destroyed in 1903, which stood further N.

Córdoba was the site of the first Talmudic school in Europe, established by Hasdai ibn Shaprut, who also promoted a curious and strange controversy on the literary use of Hebrew by the two great poets *Dunash ibn Labrat* and *Menahem ibn Soreq.*

Soon after its reconquest in 1236, the ecclesiastical authorities complained of the excessive height of the *(Rambam) Synagogue* then under construc-

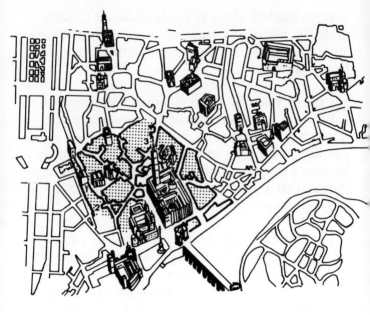

Córdoba
1. *Synagogue.*
2. *Tiberias Square and Rambam Memorial.*
3. *Location of ritual baths.*

tion, which, in a mudéjar style, was completed in 1315 (5075), and still stands, just SE of the Puerta de Almodóvar. It is said to have been built by *Isaac Moheb ben Ephraim.*

The interior walls of the building, and the women's gallery of three arcades over the entrance, are embellished with quotations from the Psalms. After the expulsion of 1492 it was converted into the church if *San Crispín.* The original artesonado ceiling was replaced by vaults in the 18C. Its dependencies were probably a Talmudic school. It was also known as the church of *Santa Quiteria.*

The community was at one time largely engaged in the manufacture and marketing of textiles, but they were decimated in the riots of 1391, and although there was a partial revival in the 15C, many Conversos were obliged to flee into the Sierra during anti-semitic attacks in 1473-74; while those who remained suffered considerably at the hands of the Inquisition established there in 1482, and which remained active until the 18C. Among the more ferocious of the inquisitors was *Diego Rodríguez Lucero* —from 1499 to 1509.

From the Puerta de Almodóvar the *Calle de Fernández Ruano* runs E through what was the commercial quarter of the Judería, off which are lanes entitled *de la Ropería* (clothiers), *Curtidoría* (tanners), *Alcaicería* (silk exchange), and *Platería* (silversmiths).

La Coruña (206,800 inhab; capital of its province), an important port, had a Jewish community in the 11C, tombstones from which epoch being now preserved in the Archaeological Museum, Madrid. The community lived in a suburb on a neck of land some distance from the old centre, immediately E of the port, and between the *Calle Juan Flórez* and the *Parque de Santa Margarita*. The site is threaded by the *Calle de A. Rabiada*. Closer to the sea on the hillock known as the *Peña dos Xudios*, stood their cemetery, now known as the *Barrio de La Palloza*, where it is said stood the synagogue.

The community expanded in the 15C, trading with Castilian and Aragonese ports, and in 1451 contributed towards the ransom of their coreligionist in Murcia. In 1476 *Joseph ibn Hayyim* here completed the illuminated «Kennicot Bible» now in the Bodleian Library, Oxford (and based on the Lisbon codex written at Cervera in 1299-1300).

Coruña
I. Harbour.
II. Orzan Bay.
1. La Palloza.
2. A Rabiada, location of Jewry.

Daroca (2700 inhab; 39 km SE of Calatayud; province of Zaragoza), a walled town of great antiquity, had a Jewish quarter prior to its reconquest in 1122, when the flourishing community was granted the same rights as Christian and Muslim residents in the charter endorsed in 1142 by *Ramón Berenguer IV*. The Jews were attacked in 1391 and again in 1414 during the Disputation of Tortosa, after which some of its more eminent members adopted Christianity. The remaining Jews were threatened, but escaped. The position of the community apparently improved, although the limits of the Judería were redefined, and there is evidence that the Conversos were reverting to Judaizing practises. After the edict of expulsion of 1492 their property was looted, and the synagogue sold.

The Judería has been identified as lying N of the main plaza close to the *Colegiata de Santa María*, which contains a 15C painting by *Yojanán de Levi*.

Elche (148,500 inhab; 24 km SW of Alicante). The mosaic floor of what is undoubtedly a synagogue of the 4C was uncovered in 1905, but little is known of the community there, apart from passing references, such as the fact that Jews there were in charge of taxing the resident Muslim community in the 14C. The site of the synagogue is near the *Puerta de Santo Polo*.

Estella (11,300 inhab; 43 km SW of Pamplona), later an important stopping-point on the pilgrim route to Santiago de Compostela, had a influential community as early as the 11C, which congregated near the citadel; and it is known that *Moses ibn Ezra*, the 12C poet, resided there at one time. In 1144 its synagogue was converted into a church, and its Judería was destroyed in the French invasion of 1265. It later partially revived, and between 1492-98 was briefly the haven of Jews exiled from Aragón and Castile.

The ancient Judería lay on the hillside to the left of the new main road leading W, just prior to entering a short tunnel. Here, the church of *Santa*

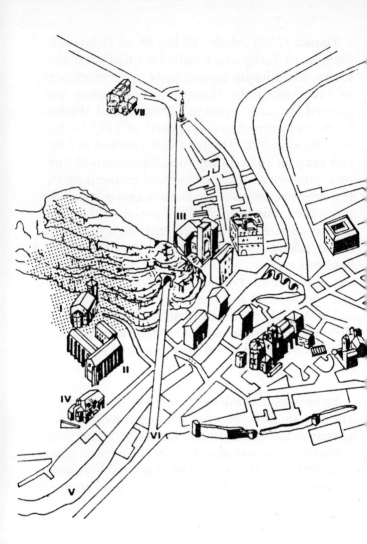

Estella
I. *Church of Santa María.*
II. *Church and convent (Dominican Orden).*
III. *Church of San Pedro de la Rúa.*
IV. *Church of the Holy Sepulchre.*
V. *River Ega.*
VI. *Old Saint James Road.*
VII. *Irache Monastery.*

María Jus del Castillo replaced a synagogue. It is also claimed that Estella had another synagogue for women only, the only instance recorded in medieval Spain.

44

Gibraltar (c. 20 km E, by road, from Algeciras), at present a British Crown Colony and naval base, lies near the narrowest part of the Straits of Gibraltar, at the W end of the Mediterranean.

The Treaty of Utrecht (1713) excluded the Jews in perpetuity, but in 1729 an agreement was reached with the Sultan of Morocco whereby Moroccan Jews were allowed to enter temporarily to trade, soon after which a community settled permanently, numbering 600 in 1749, when their legal right to remain was recognised. They then formed about one-third of the population, and had two synagogues. The Jewish cemetery is well worth visiting.

By the middle of the 19C the Jews numbered c.2000, but later dwindled. In 1980 the community, maintaining four synagogues, numbered 600 of a total population of 25,000 (including the military establishment). From 1964 its first mayor and chief minister has been *Sir Joshua A. Hassan*.

At present (1984) accession to Gibraltar from the mainland is restricted to Spanish nationals and British residents in Gibraltar.

Girona (Castilian **Gerona**; 75,100 inhab; capital of its province), Roman *Gerunda*, had an important community as early as the late 9C. It was reconquered by the Christians in 1015, and in 1160 Jews were permitted to lease shops outside the town walls. By the 13C they were taking part in the general administration of the place, although the local clergy were in the habit of celebrating Easter by bombarding the Judería with stones from the steeple of the old cathedral, for which *Pedro III* threatened to hold the bishop responsible for any damage done. At Easter 1331 the Judería, which lay immediately below the W and SW of the present *Cathedral*, was broken into by rioters. It had already suffered from French attacks in 1285, and in 1306 had absorbed a number of co-religionists expelled from France.

The community was protected after the *Disputation of Tortosa*, and in 1415 their synagogue in

the *Calle San Lorenzo* and the near by *Public Baths* were restored to them, but the former was partly destroyed during the civil war of 1462-72. By 1442, when the area of the Judería was reduced, the majority of the community had already become converted to Christianity. In 1486 the Jews there were prohibited from owning shops with doors or windows facing the main street. Six years later the majority of those remaining chose exile, their property being sold off.

In the mid 13C it became the first centre of Kabbalism in Spain, and produced a number of scholars, many taking the name «Gerondi», one of whom was related to Nahmanides.

In *Sant Pere de Galligans,* to the N of the Cathedral, on the far side of a rivulet, and now the

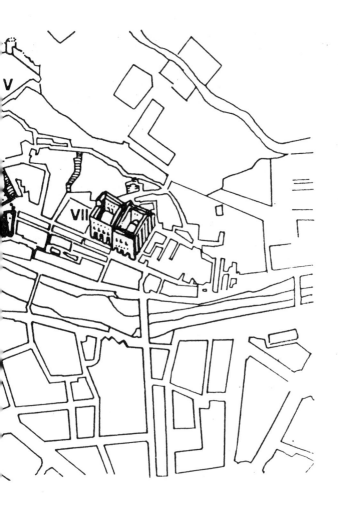

Girona
I.   Cathedral.
II.   Sobre Portes Gate location.
III.   Church of San Félix.
IV.   Roman wall (non-existent).
V.   Dominican convent.
VI.   Church of San Nicolás.
VII.   Town Hall.
VIII. La Pía Almoina.
IX.   Oña River.
X.   Archeological Museum.
1.   Probable location of Synagogue.
2.   Traditional location of Synagogue.
3.   Cervantes Street.
4.   Clavería Street and Steps.
5.   Ballesterías Street.
6.   Montjuic Park (Jewish cementery).
7.   Arab and (Jewish) baths.

Archaeological Museum, are a number of tomb-stones taken from the Jewish cemetery of *Mont-juic,* which stood further N on the hillside.

In 1982 reconstruction was completed of an area reputed to have been the house of Kabbalist *Isaac el Cec* (Blind Isaac). It lies in what is believed to be the heart of the medieval Call.

Granada (214,200 inhab; capital of its province) was anciently settled by Jews, and even the Moors assumed that they had been the founders of what they called *Gharnata' al-Yahud* (Granada of the Jews), but they are first referred to as forming part of the garrison after its conquest by the Arabs in 711. (But see also *Elvira*). Its important community had a considerable share in its administration in the 11C, *Samuel ha-Nagid* (or *Ibn Nagre-lla;* died 1055) being both vizier and military commander of the independent state, then controlled by Berbers, who preferred to depend on a Jew rather than a rival Arab party. Samuel ibn Nagrella was a distinguished scholar and a patron of the arts. Among his protegés were *Yehudah Halevi, Salomon ibn Gabirol* and *Moses ibn Ezra.* It has been estimated that the Jews provided 20 per cent of its resident population of c.26,000. *Joseph ha-Nagid* (Samuel's son) was killed in a mass revolt in 1066, but although the community revived briefly, it virtually perished when the city was taken by *Ibn Tashfin* the Almoravid, in 1090. Among the refugees was the Ibn Ezra family.

Only Jews who converted to Islam were permitted to live there during the Almohad regime (1148-1212). Both Jews and Mozarabs previously expelled returned there during the rule of the Nasrid dynasty (1232-1492), their numbers being increased by an influx of Conversos after 1391, where they openly reverted to Judaism.

Although agreeing to protect the Jews of Granada prior to its surrender, once the city was in their hands the Catholic Kings signed the *Edict of Expulsion* there (Alhambra, Ambassadors Hall, 31 March 1492), and shortly after its 20,000 resident Jews (according to a contemporary German trave-

Granada
I. Los Tiros House.
II. Torres Bermejas.
III. Girones House.
IV. Dominican Convent.
V. Puerta Real (Royal Gate).
VI. Church of San Matías.
VII. Coal Corral (Old Arab market).
VIII Carmelitan Convent.
IX Diputación Provincial.
X Church of Santa Catalina.
XI Cathedral.
1. Old Alhambra (probable palace of Samuel Hanagid).
2. Los Tiros Square (centre of Jewry).

ller, Jeronimus Münzer) left for North Africa, the Judería was razed on the orders of Fernando.

Although the Judería probably covered a considerably more extensive area at the time, it centered on an area S and E of the *Corral del Carbón*, and was overlooked by the *Torres Bermejas*.

Guadalajara (45,050 inhab; capital of its province) had a Jewish community under the Visigoths, who when the place was captured by *Tariq* in 714, were entrusted with its later defence. In 1085 *Joseph Ferruziel (Cidellus)* of Guadalajara was physician to *Alfonso VI*.

Moisés de León (1240-1305), author of the *Sefer ha-Zohar* (1274), was born there.

Segregation was imposed on the community in 1391.

A Hebrew printing-press was set up there in 1482, which produced the earliest known printed example of the *Aggada*. It was the birthplace of Rabbi *Moses Arragel,* first translator of the Bible into Castilian (see *Maqueda*). Also at this period *Isaac Abravanel* (or Abarbanel) resided there, and Guadalajara, with one of the highest tax assessments in the country, was an important Jewish cultural centre.

At the expulsion, most of the Jews of Guadalajara left for North Africa. There were then four synagogues of importance remaining in the town, the main one adjacent to the church of *San Pedro y San Pablo,* while their cemetery is said to have been in the vicinity of the *Calle de Madrid* and the present *Hospital provincial*. The Jewish quarter extended —in the N. of the town— between the streets today called del *Ingeniero Mariño* and del *Dr Benito Hernando*. In the centre of this area, and between the abovementioned streets, lies the *Calle de la Sinagoga*.

Guadalupe (3000 inhab; 82 km E of Trujillo). Its community revived after the pogrom of 1391, but were forbidden to remain there after 1485. The Conversos, many of whom relapsed, continued to reside in the old Judería, and several entered the neighbouring monastery of *San Bartolomé de Lupiana,* two monks of which were burned at the stake for converting to Judaism. Meanwhile the famous Jeronomite *Convent* at Guadalupe had also become a refuge for Marranos.

Ecija (33,400 inhab; 51 km SW of Córdoba). *Joseph de Ecija (Joseph ha-Levi ibn Shabbat)* distinguished himself in the service of *Alfonso XI* of Castile, but in 1391 its synagogue was destroyed by the fanatic archdeacon, *Ferrant Martínez,* who had in Seville provoked the destructive pogrom of that year by his violent anti-semitic preaching. It community revived later, and it is known that a group of Conversos under the leadership of *Fernando de Trujillo* (himself a Converso) resided there in 1477.

Hervás (3550 inhab.; 70 km N of Cáceres). An important medieval Jewish centre, often mentioned in the context of financial matters of the Castilian crown. The Jewish quarter stood at the NW end of the town behind the fortress-church, and sited at a lower level; it is still clearly identifiable today. One of the main streets of the quarter is called *Calle del Rabilero* (Rabbi's street) connected with *Calle de la Sinagoga.* No. 1 of the latter street is reputed to have housed the synagogue. At one end of the quarter stands the *Casa de los Diezmos* (House of the Tithes) where Jews paid their taxes. The next house holds a tiled inscription in Spanish and Hebrew dedicated by the Madrid chapter of Amistad Judeo-cristiana.

Even if most of the local traditions are not supported by scientific evidence, it is remarkable how the local population shows their attachment to their Jewish past, which they claim to hold in great honour and respect.

By the bridge over the *Ambrón* river one can see an odd-looking carved rock known as the *Knight.* Local lore claims that it was a monument erected to the massive conversion to Christianity of local Jews.

Huesca
I.   *Jewry.*
II. *Moorish quarter.*
III. *Cathedral.*
IV. *Church of San Pedro el Viejo.*
V.   *Probable location of synagogue.*
VI. *Probable location of Jewry Square.*

Huesca (36,500 inhab; capital of its province) had an important Jewish community —largely active in the cloth and silk trade— prior to the Christian reconquest of the city in 1096; but it declined in the 14C, having suffered in the riots of 1320. Its Jews were likewise persecuted during the Black Death (1348-49); accused of stealing a Host in 1377; and although protected during the general pogrom of 1391, repressive measures against the community increased after the *Disputation of Tortosa.*

Conversos from Castile settled there in 1465, and reverted to Judaism, for which some were burned at the stake by order of the Inquisition in the 1480s. Those remaining were expelled in 1492, after their gold and silver had been confiscated, and after guards had been posted in the Judería to ensure that property was not sold without the authorisation of the commissioners appointed to supervise the expulsion.

The Judería itself, which once contained three synagogues, stood on the lower NE slope of the old town centre, to the E of what is now the *Calle Joaquín Costa* and abutting the *Calle Pedro IV*. In the early 14C the community occupied 108 houses; the Moors 69. Their cemetery is referred to in 1156.

Jaca (10,300 inhab; 11km E of Pamplona). There was a community here in the mid 11C, which had settled in the *Ciudadela de San Marcos,* but it was annihilated during the massacre of 1320. It partially revived, only to have its Judería burned down in 1391, and its few remaining Jews were expelled in 1492. It had two synagogues.

Játiva (**Xátiva**; 22,400 inhab; 59 km, S W of Valencia). The Jewish quarter was restored to the community after the capture of the town by *Jaime I of Aragón* in 1244, although in 1268 the king had to forbid the practice of stoning the Jews on Good Friday. A centre for the study of Hebrew and Arabic was established here in 1291 by the Dominicans; and it has been suggested that the paper mill of Játiva, perhaps the oldest in Europe, had been a Jewish enterprise.

Among its natives was the pioneer Hebrew printer *Solomon Zalmati.*

A section of plaster retaining some Hebrew writing, probably from a synagogue, is preserved in the *Municipal Museum.*

Jerez de la Frontera (167,000 inhab; 34 km NE of Cádiz) had an ancient and important community of Jews when reconquered in 1255, which was extended by an influx of Jews from Castile who were granted property there. The Judería lay near the *Calle de San Cristóbal*, running parallel to the town wall, and contained two synagogues. Largely occupied with viticulture and general commerce, the community was exempted from certain customs duties, etc., as confirmed in 1332. They then numbered some 90 families. They were attacked in 1391, but later revived, although 50 citizens became Conversos.

The Conversos who had fled from the town in 1481 had their property confiscated by the Inquisition. The remaining Jews endeavoured to sell their property in 1483, but the local authorities prohibited people from buying it. The community had ceased to exist by 1485. Autos-de-fé were held here in 1491-92, and many Jews passed through the town en route for North Africa after the edict of expulsion of that latter year. One of its two synagogues was destroyed in 1479.

Adjacent to the *Puerta de Sevilla* is a lane known as «*de la Sinagoga*» or «de la Judería».

León (113,300 inhab; capital of its province, and previously of the ancient kingdom of León). The earliest sources refer to a *Castro Judeorum* in the vicinity of *Puente Castro,* to the E of the present centre, and the original site of the inscribed tombstones (11C), some of which can be seen in the provincial *Museum* housed in the *Hospital de San Marcos.*

The main Judería the appears to have been situated SW of the *Plaza Mayor* towards the church of *Nuestra Señora del Mercado,* with a later extension S towards *Santa Ana.* The Jews of León, being under royal jurisdiction, received certain privileges. In 1293 *King Sancho* agreed to the exclusion of Jews from tax-farming in León under pressure from the Cortes of Valladolid, and from this period their importance declined. In the mid 14C they were compelled to wear a distinctive yellow badge.

In 1449 the Judería was attacked and pillaged, but the community was later (in 1485) allowed to

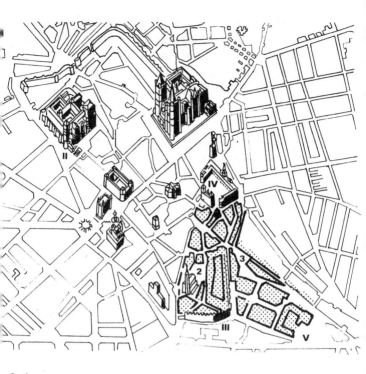

León
I. Cathedral.
II. Church of San Isidoro.
III. Old walls.
IV. Plaza Mayor (Main Square).
V. Santa Ana Square.
1. Mulacín Street.
2. Santa María del Camino Square.
3. Caño de Santa Ana Square.

enlarge the district, although earlier in the decade there had been a move to disperse them. Their property was seized on the expulsion of 1492, but returned to those few who accepted baptism.

It is suggested that No 10 in the *Calle de la Misericordia*, leading towards the *Plaza del Caño de Santa Ana*, may have been the site of the main synagogue. The activities of the Jews of León were largely commercial, particularly in the manufacturing and marketing of cloth, but they also owned vineyards in the vicinity of the capital.

Lérida (**Lléida** in Catalan; 100,900 inhab; capital of its province) had a Jewish community from the 11C, whose Judería was located in the parish of *San Andrés* (the church is just opposite the bottom of the flight of steps descending W from the fortified enceinte in which stands the Cathedral).

Members of the community were largely occupied in tanning, but among them were some merchants and a few farmers. In 1173 one of their synagogues was converted into a church *(Santa María del Miracle,* or *El Milagro)*. Some Jews from Lérida settled in Valencia after its capture in 1238.

There were several reversions to Judaism among the Conversos of Lérida in the early 14C. During the massacres following the Black Death (1348) the community was forced to seek safety in the citadel. In 1383 two of them were accused of desecrating the Host, a not uncommon accusation at the time. In 1391 some 78 of their number were slaughtered, and the Judería was destroyed; but although the Jews were re-establised during the following decade, they hardly flourished, in spite of being granted privileges. Meanwhile its Conversos were allowed the use of the church previously a synagogue. In 1490 a tribunal of the Inquisition was established there, and in 1514 an unsuccessful attempt was made to assassinate the Inquisitor.

Lucena (29,400 inhab; 73 km S of Córdoba) in the 11C had one of the most important and influential communities in Andalucía, which developed in the following century into an academic and cultural centre. Indeed during the Muslim period it was sometimes known as «Lucena of the Jews», as confirmed by the Arab geographer *Idrisi,* who remarked that only Jews lived within the fortified area, although some Muslims resided without the walls. Their activities were mainly commercial and agricultural, and they owned olive-groves and vineyards in the vicinity.

Lucena had one of the first Talmudic schools in Europe, which was founded by *Isaac Alfassi,* who died here in 1103. He was followed by *Yosef ibn Migash. Salomon ibn Gabirol, Yehudah Halevi,* and *Maimonides*'s father studied there.

There was an uprising of Jews in Lucena in c.1090, probably against the Almoravides, and a decade later the Almoravide ruler demanded that they convert to Islam. They were only able to save themselves by paying extortionate bribes. Nevertheless, many were forced to convert during the Almohad wars (1146) and never really recovered their influence after this period. It was conquered by Castile in 1240, and as with so many other places in Andalucía, its fate was sealed by the massacres of 1391.

There is circumstantial evidence that the present church of *Santiago* may have been once the main synagogue. Local people are referring increasingly to that church as *la Sinagoga.*

Madrid (3,228,000 inhab; the capital of Spain and of its province) was of very slight importance until the 13C, a Cortes meeting there for the first time in 1309. A small Jewish community was already there in the 11C, which remained after its capture by *Alfonso VI* in 1083. The main Judería was situated between the present *Calle de Bailén* (to the W), the present *Plaza de Oriente* (which was previously —until the early 19C— a maze of alleys), the *Plaza de Isabel II* (to the N), the *Calle Mayor* to the S, and the *Calle Santiago* to the E in the proximity of the old *Puerta de Vallmandú.*

A smaller Judería perhaps existed around the *Plaza de Lavapiés,* some distance S of the *Puerta del Sol,* the centre of the old town, and by the *Calle de la Fe.* The synagogue was destroyed in the rioting of 1391, and the community never entirely recovered. Many adopted Christianity, but these Conversos were attacked for their judaizing tendencies in the early 1460s, led by *Alfonso de Espina* and *Alonso de Oropesa.* Jews were also prohibited from trading in foodstuffs and medicaments, and from practicing as surgeons. Some Conversos were later tried at Toledo, but when Madrid became the capital in 1561, the supreme tribunal of the Inquisition was moved there, and numerous *autos-de-fe* were «celebrated» in the *Plaza Mayor*. Between 1580 and 1640 a number of Portuguese Jews settled in Madrid, some of them also aprehended by the Holy Office, and likewise tried.

After 1869 Jews were able to settle freely in Madrid, but it was not until the 1920s that the community was in any way organised. It was the asylum for some Jewish refugees during the First World War, and again in the early 1930s. In 1941 the *Arias Montano Institute for Jewish Studies* was founded, together with a department in the University of Madrid, and in the late 1960s a Jewish centre and *Synagogue* was built at No 3 *Calle Balmes,* not far from the *Plaza de Sorolla*. By then the community numbered over 3000.

Some Jewish tombstones removed from Toledo may be seen in the *Archaeological Museum*.

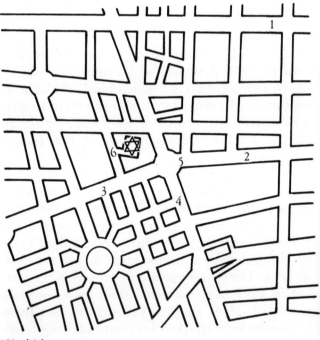

Madrid

1. *Calle José Abascal.*
2. *Calle General Martínez Campos.*
3. *Calle Eloy Gonzalo.*
4. *Calle Santa Engracia.*
5. *Plaza de Sorolla.*
6. *Calle Balmes. (Synagogue)*

Majorca (Cast. *Mallorca),* the largest of the Balearic Islands, was on important Mediterranean trading routes, and Jewish settlements there date back to the 4-5Cs, but they may well have been destroyed when the islands were taken by *Belisarius* in 534. Presumably some Jews as well as Christians fled there from Andalucía at the commencement of the Moorish invasion (711), but the earliest evidence from this period is dated 1135, when *Ramón Berenguer II,* Count of Barcelona, took some Majorcan Jews under his protection.

Jaime I conquered the island in 1229-32, and property was distributed among the several Jews in his retinue; while in *Palma,* the capital, a district was set aside for them in the fortress of *Almudaina.* The community was soon after enlarged by the arrival of Jews from the South of France, North Africa, and even as far afield as Alexandria, and the extension of their residential quarters led to disputes.

There were communities on the island at *Inca, Petra, Montiori, Felanitx, Sineu, Alcudia, Sóller,* and *Pollensa,* among other villages. Their rights and considerable privileges were confirmed in 1250, but although they prospered materially, it was also confirmed (in 1273) that they should live separate from Christians, and the Judería in Palma from then on lay between the *Calles de Temple* and *de Calatrava* to the E of the Cathedral, and centered on the *Calle del Sol.*

Ramón Llull (c.1235-c.1316), the poet and theologian, and a native of the island, is said to have engaged in disputes with the Jews at this period. Later their situation deteriorated. There were anti-Jewish riots there in 1305 and 1309, and in the following years a number of prohibitive regulations concerning them were issued. Their synagogue in Palma was confiscated and converted into a church, but they were later allowed to erect a new one less splendid than the old. Meanwhile, the neighbouring island of *Minorca* —see below— had been recaptured, in 1287. After 1343, when *Pedro IV* took control of the Balearics, the condition of the Jewish community improved, and their privileges were reconfirmed; but with the outbreaks of plague in the next few decades they were the object of persecution. It was at this period that the Jewish school of cartographers and astronomers flourished on the island, among the most eminent being *Abraham Cresques* (d.1387), and his son *Judah*. A monument to *Abraham Cresques* has been recently erected on the waterfront of *Palma*.

Although the viceroy endeavoured to protect the community during the 1391 riots, the Judería in Palma was attacked and a number of Jews killed. The communities at Sóller, Sineu, and Alcudia

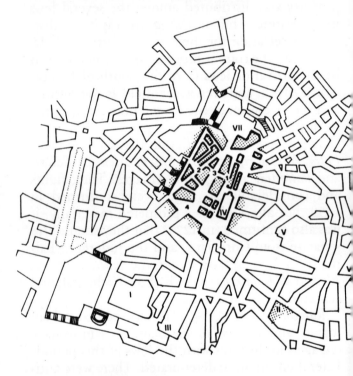

Palma de Mallorca
I.   *Cathedral*
II.   *Montesión Church*
III. *Bishops Palace*
IV.   *Santa Eulalia Church*
V.   *Franciscan Convent*
VI.   *Former Templar Church*
VII. *Main Square*
1.   *Platerías Street*
2.   *Jaime II Street (formerly Segell Street)*
3.   *Colón Street (formerly Bunyols Street)*
4.   *Cort Square*

were wiped out. A number were ostensibly convert-ed, but many others emigrated, mostly to North Africa. In 1413 the island was visited by *Vicent Ferrer,* and further conversions followed, but by 1435 the Jewish community in Majorca had ceas-ed to exist.

The Conversos of Majorca were known as *Chue-tas,* and they continued to live in a separate quart-er (between the *Plaza de Cort* and *Plaza Mayor* of Palma), but the Inquisition was active among them from 1488 to 1520, and again in 1675-77, and 1691. By 1771 they had sent a total of 594 Chuetas to the stake. In 1782 they were permit-ted to settle anywhere in the town or island, and al-though they were granted further concessions, they were discriminated against in 1856. But in gen-eral they have since carried on their activities un-disturbed. In 1970 there remained some 300 mem-bers of this community in Palma, largely silver-smiths, whose church is *Santa Eulalia:* there are probably many more on the island.

Among other sites possibly of Jewish origin are the so-called *Baños árabes* (11C) in the Calle de Serra; the *Capilla de Santa Fe* in the Calle de las Platerías, and the church of *San Bartolomé,* both, it has been claimed, on the sites of synagogues. Nearby *Calle de los Estudios* refers to ancient location of the rabinical schools.

Little is known of the Jews of *Minorca,* although there are early references to them —such as the apologetical letter by Bishop Sever (417)—, when in the 5C their community at *Mahon* was attack-ed, their synagogue was destroyed, and they were forced to accept baptism, becoming in fact the first Conversos.

Their later history is closely connected with Ma-jorca, and they and the Jews of *Ibiza,* were includ-ed in the taxes levied by the communal leaders in Palma. The community was considerably depleted by the Black Death (1348), and any remaining judaizers were sentenced by the Inquisition of Majorca, although another small community flourished there again during the temporary English occupation of the island in the mid 18C.

Málaga (408,450 inhab; capital of its province) had a community during the Moslem occupation, who settled just W of the slope of *Gibralfaro,* on which stood the citadel. The Judería lay between the pesent *Calle San Agustín* (in which stands the Museo de Bellas Artes) and the *Alcazabilla,* and from the *Plaza de la Merced* to the N to the *Plaza de la Aduana.* It was a refuge in 1013 for *Samuel ibn Nagrella,* when the Berbers captured Córdoba, and here in c.1021 was born *Salomon ben Judah ibn Gabirol,* also known as *Avicebron,* The poet and philosopher, whose statue may be seen here.

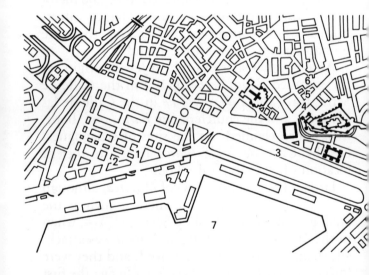

Málaga

1.   *Avenida de Córdoba.*
2.   *Calle Duquesa de Parcent. (Synagogue)*
3.   *Paseo del Parque.*
4.   *Alcazabilla.*
5.   *Ibn Gabirol Memorial.*
6.   *Probable site of last Jewry.*
7.   *Harbour.*

The *Calle de Santa Ana,* and parallel *Calle del Muro de Santa Ana,* leading SE of the Plaza de la Merced, were also probably part of the Judería after the reconquest of the city in 1487, when some 100 families were taken captive, and ransomed by *Abraham Senior* and *Salomon ibn Verga,* among others. They were forced to leave the port three years later, unless they converted to Christianity. Those who left, it is said, were captured on the high seas by Basque pirates.

Medina del Campo (17,350 inhab; 43 km SW of Valladolid), one of the most important market towns of the plain (a wheat belt), as its name implies, had a Jewish prosperous community in the 13C, who survived heavy taxation, and in the following century still counted up to 100 householders, but it suffered under the anti-semitic regulations promulgated at Zamora in 1313.

It had a flourishing Converso community in the 15C, among whom a campaign was launched by *Alonso de Espina,* when it was found that some 30 were circumcised. One physician then circumcised himself, and fled to Israel. Its last rabbi, *Isaac Uzziel,* left in 1492, and settled at Salonica.

Miranda de Ebro (35,600 inhab; 35 km SW of Vitoria). The Jews of Miranda were given equal rights with Moorish and Christian residents in the *fuero* or charter of 1099, but the community was comparatively small. They were virtually massacred in 1360 by supporters of Enrique de Trastámara. Those who survived left in 1492, when their synagogue —preserved in a house at No 18 *Calle de la Puente*— was handed over to the municipality. The Judería lay in the vicinity of the *Calle de la Independencia.*

Near the railway station stood a camp were thousands of Jewish and non-Jewish refugees were concentrated during II World War. Nothing remains of the camp.

Monzón (14,200 inhab; 50 km NW of Lérida) had a community dating back to the second half of the 12C. Together with neighbouring communities it experienced anti-semitic riots in 1260, and again in 1348 after the Black Death, when they there were forced to seek refuge within the walled enclave. They survived the 1391 persecutions virtually unharmed, although were some conversions. Two representatives were sent to the *Disputation of Tortosa* in 1413-14, one result of which was that their synagogue was converted into the church of *El Salvador*. The majority of the community is said to have been converted at this time, but there must have been a revival, for the records of the 1460-70s mention the names of 44 Jewish householders. The synagogue lamp is preserved in the *Provincial Museum* at Zaragoza.

Morella (3300 inhab; 60 km W of Vinaroz, province of Castellón) was settled by Jews in 1264, when *Jaime I* of Aragón granted them privileges similar to those accorded to the Jews of Valencia. Their Judería was said to have been in the district known as «*del Públich*», between the church of *San Miguel* and the *Plaza de Toros,* but claims have also been made that it lay between the *Calles de Don Blasco de Alagón* and *de San Juan*, and traversed by the *Calle San Nicolás,* but no visible proofs are extant.

Medinaceli (1200 inhab; 75 km S of Soria) had , a Jewish community in the 12C, who in the following century were granted the same status as Christians. Its synagogue is assumed to have been the present church of *San Román,* the keys of which are available from the local priest. The large salt pans in the lower valley —still in use— were once owned and exploited by the Jews up to the expulsion of 1492, and later by Conversos.

Nájera (5600 inhab; 26 km SW of Logroño) had an ancient and at one time important community, which enjoyed a municipal charter early the 11C, which served as model for later *fueros* in the area, and in which the blood price specified for a Jew

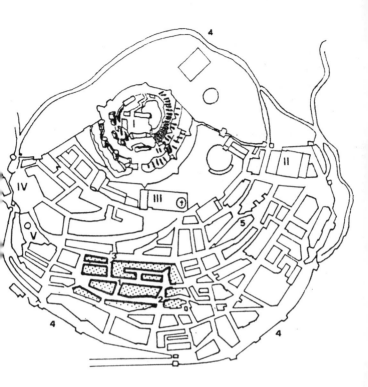

Morella

I.   Castle
II.   San Miguel Church
II.   Church of the Archpriest
IV.   Main Square
V.   Colón Square
1.   San Nicolás Street
2.   San Juan Street
3.   Don Blasco de Aragón Street
4.   City Walls
5.   Old Moorish quarter

was equal to that paid for killing a member of the clergy or a knight.

The community, which lived between the market-place and the wall at the S side of the town, around the convent of *Santa María la Real,* owned property in the town and vineyards in the district, but suffered considerably during the civil wars between *Pedro the Cruel* and *Enrique de Trastámara,* particularly after the battle near by (1367), in which the *Black Prince* defeated Enrique. Little is known of the community between then and its eventual expulsion the following century. The choir-stalls of Santa María la Real are claimed to have been carved by Converso craftsmen; likewise the door leading from the choir to the cloister.

Oña (1,500 inhab.; 20 km NW of Briviesca). The Jewish is easily located by passing through the *Arco de la Estrella* towards *Plaza Mayor*.

To the left of the Arch is *Calle Barruso*, the former main street of the Judería.

The second house on the right-hand side with an overhanging storey was, according to tradition —supported by a document of 1405—, a synagogue.

Orense (80,200 inhab; capital of its province). A Jewish settlement of the 11C is recorded, and the community lived near the fortress. The Judería lay between the *Rúa Nova*, and the *Calles del Instituto* and *del Obispo Cesáreo*, but it was later transferred to the neighbourhood of the *Fuente del Obispo*. In 1489 the governor of Galicia was ordered by the Catholic Kings to protect the Jews of Orense, but three years later they were expelled.

Palencia (62,200 inhab; capital of its province) had a flourishing community which probably existed prior to the first reference to them in 1175. The Judería lay in the old parish of *San Julián*, between the church of *San Miguel*, and near the river Carrión, but this was destroyed in 1391.

In 1480 the remaining Jews were obliged to live in a new quarter separate from the Conversos, and this was in the Calle María Gutiérrez (now *Calle Martín Calleja)*. After their expulsion, the street was re-named *Santa Fe*, and a fine was imposed on anyone referring to it as the Judería. In 1485 the Jews were ordered to wear a distinctive badge. In 1492 a synagogue once sited in the present *Calle de San Marcos* was sold, the proceeds paying to assist the departure of the refugees; another synagogue was converted into a hospital. Nothing remains to recall the Jewish community; even those tombstones preserved in the *Provincial Museum*

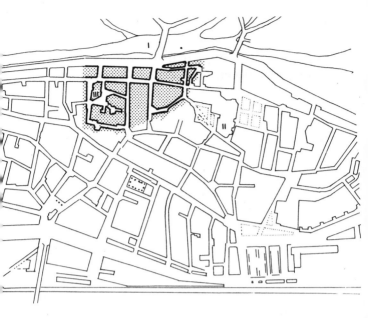

Palencia
I.   *Carrión River.*
II.   *Cathedral.*
III.   *Church of San Miguel.*

come from the neighbouring town of *Paredes de Nava*.

Pamplona (163,200 inhab; capital of Navarre). A Jewish community here is referred to in the early 10C. In 958 it was visited by *Hasdai ibn Shaprut*, at which time the Judería was located in an area known as the *Navarrería*, but this was sacked and Jewish property confiscated in riots during the 1270s. The community survived nevertheless, and was granted certain privileges.

A dispute took place here in 1375 between *Pedro de Luna* (who later became the anti-pope Benedict XIII: see **Tortosa**) and *Shem Tov ibn Isaac Shaprut*. By 1400 there were over 200 Jewish families resident, partially increased by the influx of refugees from Castile after the progroms of 1391. *Carlos III* of Navarre instituted certain restrictions. The community survived a plague in 1401-11, but in 1469 were ordered to reside only within their Judería. For some six years after 1492 some Jews from Castile sought protection here, until the general order of expulsion from Navarre was promulgated. Nothing remains of the Judería, which was sited between the *Cathedral*, the *Walls*, and the *Plaza del Castillo*.

Plasencia (28.000 inhab; 79 km N of Cáceres). The Jewish quarter in the suburb of *Jaraiz* prospered in the 13C, but was discriminated against in 1313. By the end of the 14C it still had some 50 householders. An auto-de-fe was held there in 1489, and three years later, at the expulsion, their synagogue was converted into the church of *Santa Isabel*, which was burned down during the rebellion of the Comuneros early in the 16C.

Ribadavia (6600 inhab, 29 km W of Orense). It is estimated that in the 14C the local Jewish population was 1500. The town was a major trading centre in the Middle Ages both for cattle and fish. In 1386 the town was under siege by the Black Prince and the Jews were in charge of the defence of two gates: *Porta Nova* and *Porta do Arrabal*. As a punishment the Jewish quarter was the only one destroyed by the English troops when the town was conquéred.

The Jewry was located in the area between the Porta Nova (New Gate) and the *Church of Santiago*, and between the *Plaza de la Magdalena* and the of the old walls, by the riverside.

Sagunto (at one time known as *Murviedro;* 52,000 inhab; 27 km N of Valencia), Roman *Saguntum*, had a Jewish community when captured by *Jaime I* of Aragón; the Vives family were given a bakery there for services rendered during the siege. The Judería lay on the W side of the *Roman Theatre*, centered on the *Calles Segovia* and *Ramos*, and in 1321 they were given permission to fortify it. Seven years later they acquired ground for a new cemetery, tombstones from which are preserved in the *Museum*. The fortified Judería

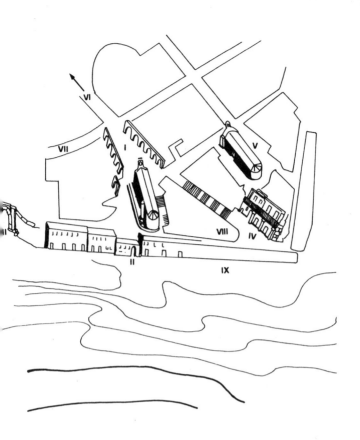

Ribadavia
I.   *Magdalena Church and Square*
II.   *Arrabal Gate*
III. *Porta Nova (New Gate)*
IV. *Jewish houses*
V.   *Santiago Church*
VI. *Road to Town Hall*
VII. *Bodegas Street*
VIII. *Possible location of Synagogue*
IX. *Houses built on site of old walls*

protected them during the pogrom of 1391, after which the privileged community continued to flourish, and, it has been suggested, encouraged Conversos to return to Judaism.

There are references to the fact that at the expulsion many of the community sailed either to Oran in North Africa, or Naples, while their synagogue in the present *Calle de la Sangre Vieja* was converted into the church of *Sangre de Cristo*. It

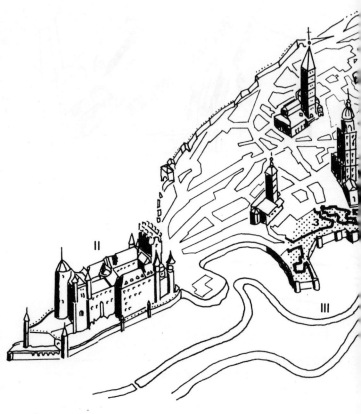

Segovia
I. Cathedral.
II. Alcázar.
III. Walls.
IV. Aqueduct.
V. Los Hoyos Hill.
VI. Hontanillas Hill.
1. Jewish cemetery.
2. Old Jewry.
3. New Jewry.

has also been argued that the arch of No. 2, *Calle de Antigones* is possibly the remains of another synagogue.

At *Benavites*, 7 km N of Sagunto, there stands a 15C tower; in its construction a number of tomb-

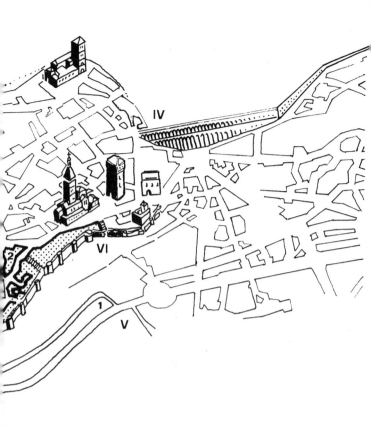

stones from Sagunto's Jewish cemetery were used. Some of the stones show Hebrew inscriptions.

Segovia (46,950 inhab; capital of its province) had a prosperous community in the 13C, with its Judería just S of the present *Cathedral —Calle de la Judería—* and extending along the S wall of the old town, and later further to the W, but it suffered during the civil wars of the next century, and by 1390 only some 50 families remained. In 1391, although *Enrique III* was then residing there, he was apparently unable to protect the Jews, and although the community later recovered, it never again prospered.

In 1412 Queen *Catherine of Lancaster* ordered the Jews to be confined to a new area still known as the *Barrio Nuevo* or *Judería Nueva*, where the present church of *La Merced* is believed to have been the synagogue. In 1415 they were accused with the desecration of the Host; and in the 1480s Segovia became a centre of anti-semitic and anti-Converso activity, some of it incited by *Antonio de la Peña,* whose excesses were the subject of a complaint by *Abraham Senior,* who did much to protect the community, which at that time was offering shelter to co-religionists expelled from Andalucía. At this period a number of important tax-farmers were resident there, including Senior and his son-in-law, *Meir Melamed* Both of them converted to Christianity in 1492, retained all their privileges, and adopted the family name of *Coronel,* which was later linked with the families of the local nobility.

Its main synagogue had been confiscated and converted into the church of *Corpus Christi* by 1420. It stands on the S side ot the upper end of the *Calle Juan Bravo,* leading up from the *Aqueduct* to the *Plaza Mayor,* and was probably built during the 13C in the Mudéjar style, and has certain resemblences to Santa María la Blanca at Toledo, but is much plainer in detail. In 1572 it became the property of Franciscan nuns, and was very seriously damaged by fire in 1899, after which it was tastelessly restored.

An ancient cemetery is said to have been in the valley of the Clamores below the town walls once buttressing the Judería, at a site known as *El Fonsario.*

Salamanca (131,400 inhab; capital of its province) had a thriving community during the 13C, with one synagogue located in the *Calle Postigo Ciego,* but in 1335 it suffered from discriminatory regulations, for Christians were forbidden to receive medical attention from Jews, etc., nor were Jews allowed to rent houses near churches and Christian cemeteries. The Judería was largely destroyed in 1391, and in 1411-12 during *Vicent Ferrer's* visit to the university city, one of the synagogues was converted into the church of *la Vera Cruz.* The Judería lay between the Bishop's Palace and the Roman Bridge.

The community was libelled in 1456 for a ritual

murder, but was saved from attack by royal intervention. In 1480 *Abraham Zacut,* a native of Salamanca, became astronomer to the bishop. There was a massive migration of Salmantine Jews into Portugal in 1474.

Sepúlveda (1800 inhab; 59 km NE of Segovia) had a prosperous community in the 13C, and were given certain privileges in 1305, including that of having their own cemetery in exchange for a tax on pepper. Nevertheless, any Christian women who nursed a Jewish or Moorish child was likely to be flogged and driven from the town. The property of a *Pedro Laínez,* who returned there to convert to Christianity in 1494, was returned to him.

Seville (Sevilla in Spanish; 589,700 inhab; capital of its province) is said to have had a Jewish community from a very early period, against whom *Isidore of Seville* wrote polemics. It was captured by the Moslems in 712, who placed its defence in the hands of a Jewish guard, numbers of which later settled there. The community prospered under the Ummayad dynasty, having the monopoly of dyeing, and were otherwise engaged in general commerce, or as physicians. During the 11C it was increased by the influx of refugees from Córdoba after the Berber conquest of 1013, and later by refugees from Granada.

Here resided a number of eminent members of the Abrabanel family, and those of Ibn al-Yatom, Ibn Kamneil, Ibn Mujahir, etc., and grew into a major cultural centre during the 12C, with poets and scholars such as *Meir ibn Migash,* etc. but suffered severely in the wake of the Almohade conquest, when its Judería was virtually destroyed. This lay on the W side of the city, in the present parishes of *Santa Magdalena,* and *San Lorenzo.* Another Judería extended E from the *Cathedral* and *Alcázar* towards the *Calle de Aguilas* and church of *San Esteban,* and it was surrounded by a wall. It is now generally known as the *Barrio de Santa Cruz* or *Judería.*

Here in 1378, according to probably an exagger-

Sevilla
I.   *Church of San Bartolomé.*
II. *Church of Madre de Dios.*
III. *Church of Santa María la Blanca.*
IV. *Santa Cruz Square.*

ated claim by Ferrant Martínez, were some 23
synagogues (three of them converted mosques),
which he destroyed or converted into churches;
among them that of *Santa María la Blanca* is the
best known, which had been donated to the community by Fernando III in consideration of their
behaviour on his capture of the city in 1248. The
Jews of Seville had then presented him with a
symbolic key (still to be seen in the Cathedral Trea-
sury) engraved with the words (in Hebrew): «The
King of Kings will open; the King of the Land shall
come». The silver tomb of Fernando III, «king of
the three religions», may also be seen in the cathedral, with an epitaph written in Latin, Arabic, and
Hebrew.

In 1254 two annual fairs were established in Seville, and the Jews who attended them were granted freedom of trade and exemption from taxes. The elders of the community had nevertheless to pay tithes and taxes. By the end of the 13C some 200 Jewish families resided there.

In spite of royal instructions to the authorities to control the anti-semitic activities of *Ferrant Martínez,* the fanatical archdeacon of Ecija (87 km E), they were either incapable or connived in secret: there was no archbishop in Seville at the time. On 4 June 1391 the city erupted, and in the ensuing riots the Judería was sacked and much property destroyed. Part of the community converted, some ostensibly, others sincerely; others were killed at the outbreak of the violence, which was shortly to sweep the country. The synagogues not burnt out were converted into churches or to more mundane uses. The community never recovered from this disastrous blow, and rapidly declined. In 1476 the remaining Jews of Seville were ordered to move from the Judería into other districts, among them the *Corral de Ferez* and the *Alcázar Viejo.* Seven years later the order of expulsion of Jews from Andalucía was issued, and in 1492 Seville was a point of embarkation for refugees from western Andalucía, most of whom left for North Africa.

It had a considerable Converso community in the 15C, who continued to live in the Judería, but they were still considered as Jews, and many likewise left for Africa. *Alonso de Espina,* head of the Dominican monastery of *San Pablo,* was largely responsible for the introduction of the Inquisition into Spain, having brought to the attention of the Catholic Kings —on their visit to Seville in 1477— the serious nature of the Converso situation in undermining the purity of the Catholic Faith. In 1481 the Inquisition commenced their activities in Seville, and it has been estimated that in the next six years over 700 Conversos were burned at the stake, while over 5000 were reconciled with the Church. In 1484 a convention of Inquisitors was held here in the presence of *Torquemada* to codify their future procedures, etc.

Many Jews returned from North Africa to Seville earlier in this century, and the community was increased by refugees from Germany in the 1930s, and by others from Morocco and Algiers in the 1960s.

There is now a community of some 50 Jews.

Sigüenza (6100 inhab; 74 km NE of Guadalajara). A community probably existed there from the 11C, with their Judería lying immediately be-

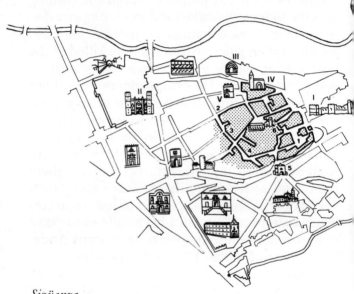

Sigüenza
I.   Castle (*Parador Nacional*).
II. Cathedral.
III. Clarisas Convent.
IV. Church of San Vicente.
V.   El Doncel House.
1.   Street of the Synagogue.
2.   San Vicente Street.
3.   Travesaña Baja.
4.   Travesía Arch.
5.   Portal Mayor (Main Gate).
6.   Puerta de Hierro (Iron Gate).

low the entrance to the castle (now the *Parador Nacional*) and between the church of *San Vicente* and the *Portal Mayor*. Its decline set in during the 15C but some Conversos remained there, being protected from derogatory expressions by a decree of 1493.

Its main synagogue, sold off in 1496, was probably that on the site of No 6 *Calle de la Sinagoga,* although this or others are referred to traditionally as being at No 12 *Calle de San Vicente.* Their cemetery lay to the W of the castle, towards the hermitage of *Santa María de las Huertas,* which was unsystematically excavated in 1826.

Soria (27,600 inhab; capital of its province) is known to have had a Jewish community during the 12C. The Judería lay on the NE side of the castle hill (on which the Parador Nacional now stands) and may have extended as far down as the present *Plaza Mayor;* and c. 1000 Jews lived there at the close of the 13C. In 1465 it was exempted from the payment of certain taxes in appreciation for services rendered to the Crown, a number of its community being important tax-farmers, but it was mulcted regularly later in the century until the expulsion of 1492, when those Jews remaining probably left for a temporary haven in Navarre. The museum of *San Juan de Duero* preserves a tombstone with a Jewish inscription.

Tarazona (11,400 inhab; 83 km NW of Zaragoza) had a thriving community, which grew in importance in the 13C, among the more influential families in which were the *Portellas,* one of whom became bailiff of Aragón. *Pedro III* protected the community, which was virtually unaffected by the persecutions of 1391, but after the *Disputation of Tortosa* there was a wave of conversion to Christianity. *Alfonso V* also attempted to rehabilitate the community (among others in Aragón), but under *Fernando V* some of its Conversos were persecuted, and the Inquisition was active there before and after the expulsion of 1492, when its remaining Jews moved to a temporary haven in adjacent Navarre.

There were two neighbouring Juderías in Tarazona, the new being merely an extension of the old, which was situated between the *Calle Conde* and the *Rúa Alta* and up to the *Puerta Ferreña,* a street by the *Episcopal Palace* still being known as «*de la Judería*», with its overhanging storeys. Its extension, after 1371, lay between the *Calle de los Aires* and the present *Plaza de la Merced*, while both sections had their individual synagogues. The Retablo de Santa Catalina, San Prudencio y San Lorenzo by the Jewish artist Yojanán de Levi of Tudela, can be seen in the *Parish Church* (see also Daroca, and Vic).

Tarragona (100,800 inhab; capital of its province) was settled by Jewish traders during the Roman era, as confirmed by an inscription, while coins of the Visigothic period with Hebrew inscriptions have also been found. Apparently it was known to the Arab geographer *Idrisi* is a «Jewish city» (mid 12C), by which time it had been reconquered by the Christians.

The Judería lay on the E side of the upper wall-

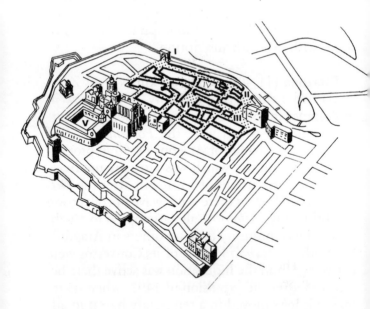

Tarragona
I.   *San Antonio Gate.*
II.   *Portella dels Jueus (Gate of the Jews).*
III.   *Archeological Museum.*
IV.   *Forat Micó.*
V.   *Cathedral and Cloister.*
VI.   *Old Jewish Square.*

ed town, between the *Cathedral* and the *Walls,* and largely between the *Puerta de San Antonio* and the Cyclopean *Puerta de la Portella* (also known as the *Portella dels Jueus*). Several Jewish tombstones of the 13-14Cs have been removed from their cemetery (which was between the old town and the *Playa de los Milagros*), and are to be seen in the *Archaelogical Museum;* other tombstones with Latin and Hebrew inscriptions are in the cathedral cloister. Another inscription can be seen on the facade of No 6 *Calle de las Escribanías Viejas.*

Archbishop *Benito de Rocaberti* obtained from Pope *Urban IV* a bull ordering the Jews of Tarragona to wear a distinguishing badge (a white circular sign), while *Clement IV* ordered the archbishop to arrange for all Jewish books in the Kingdom of Aragón to be collected at Tarragona and handed over to the Dominicans and Franciscans.

Its community was persecuted after the Black Death of 1348, and although partially protected in 1391, and measures taken for their reestablishment, they were forced to leave Spain, together with many Jews from Aragón converging on the port, in 1492.

Teruel (23,300 inhab; capital of its province) had an important community, prosperous under the Moorish occupation, and which soon recovered after the reconquest of 1171. But in general its history is of slight interest, although they experienced sporadic persecution, and occasional tax concessions. The Inquisition was active there from 1484, and in the following two years over 30 Conversos were condemned to the stake; many more were forcibly converted in 1492 at the general expulsion. The Judería is said to have been situated in the NE sector of the old town, between the *Walls* and the *Calle de Aina.*

In 1979 some remains of a construction were uncovered at the corner of the Plaza de la *Judería* and *Calle Ambeles.* Experts believe that the arches found at some 15 m below the present level may have belonged to a synagogue. Fragments of a ceramic *hanukkiya* were also found.

Toledo (51,400 inhab; 69 km SW of Madrid), capital of its province, and from the Visigothic period until 1561 capital of Spain. There was a small community here during Visigothic times, as is evident from decrees directed against the Jews by the Church Councils held there, among them that of 694, in which they were accused on no foundation of plotting with their co-religionists in North Africa to destroy the Christian kingdom. The Jewish area, which grew to cover the whole of the SW quarter of the city, and extending as far to the N as the *Puerta del Cambrón*, was surrounded by wall as early as 820. It was bisected by the *Calle de la Judería*, now the *Calle del Angel*, leading W from the present church of *El Salvador* to *San Juan de los Reyes*. It is likely that there was another smaller enclave known as the *Alcaná* nearer the cathedral (a *Calle de la Sinagoga* still exists).

Various estimates have been made as to the size of the community (which was also a centre of the Karaites in Spain), which at the height of its prosperity may have been in the region of 12,000, and they had ten synagogues, including the Great Synagogue, destroyed by fire in 1250, and the Old Synagogue, restored in 1107. Among others was that founded in 1203 by Joseph Abu 'Omar ibn Shoshan, which in 1411 was converted into the church of *Santa María la Blanca* (see below); and that known as *El Tránsito*, built c. 1357 by Meir Abdeli for Samuel Halevi (treasurer of Pedro I the Cruel, who later executed him and seized his wealth). It was transferred to the Order of Calatrava in 1494, then owned by the priory of San Benito, and later dedicated to the Dormition of the Virgin (el Tránsito).

The situation of the Jews remained virtually unchanged after Toledo was captured by Alfonso VI of Castile in 1085, continuing as a centre of translation from the Arabic into the vernacular in the fields of mathematics, astronomy, and other sciences, and thence into Latin. At this period and until the beginning of the 14C, the Jews of Toledo usually wrote in Arabic with Hebrew characters. *Joseph Ferruziel (Cidellus)* was a prominent mem-

Toledo
I.   *Santa María la Blanca Synagogue.*
II.   *El Tránsito Synagogue and Sephardic Museum.*
III.   *Casa de El Greco.*

ber of the royal court, and the Jews were in a comparatively privileged position. On Alfonso's death, however, there was a reaction against them, and in 1181 the law of 633, excluding them from holding public offices, was reintroduced. *Isaac ibn Ezra* apparently left the town in the following year, but most of the distinguished members of the community remained, among them *Moses ibn Ezra,* Ferruziel, and *Joseph ibn Camaniel,* the physician.

The community was led by seven members of the Jewish oligarchy, and a *bet din* or a rabbinical court, and from the 13C it was administered by ten *mugaddimin.* They appear to have lived in partnership with the Christians without any serious interruption until 1280, when *Alfonso X* ordered their imprisonment within their synagogues until they had paid a special tax, and attempts were made to convert them. Some years later, in 1304-05, it was the seat of controversy with regard to the works of *Maimonides;* and at about the same time the clergy of Toledo endeavoured to compel the Jews to cease their money-lending activities; but in the reign of *Alfonso XI* (1312-50) their situation improved, and *Moses Abazardiel* became a róyal scribe. The Black Death took its toll of the community in 1348, and in 1355, when Pedro the Cruel first entered the city, the Jewish quarters were attacked and many were slaughtered. By the end of the civil war they were ruined. Those who remained suffered more severely in 1391, when almost all their synagogues were set alight, and many became *Conversos* to save their skins. In 1411 *Vicent Ferrer* visited the place, where he converted the Ibn Shoshan synagogue into a church; and he is said to have converted many Jews by his preaching.

At the expulsion of 1492 most of the Toledan Jews left for Fez, North Africa, and Turkey, and two years later their remaining property was transferred to the Crown. Its large Converso community had stayed in the Jewish quearter until in the 1480s they were dispersed among Christian parishes. The Conversos had been attacked in 1449, and again in 1467, while in 1486-87 some 4000 of the inhabitants were involved in five *autos-de-fe,* in which some were burnt at a site now the *Plaza de Zocodover.* The Inquisition continued there for many decades. Among those sentenced by it was *Alvaro de Montalbán,* father of Fernando de Rojas, author of *La Celestina.*

After decades of neglect, the *Sinagoga del Tránsito* was partially restored at the instigation of *Francisco Pérez Bayer,* a priest, in the mid 17C, and the women's gallery and other sections have been since restored. The interior has no aisles. Note the Moorish arcade, the frieze displaying the arms of Castile and León; the arabesques; and the Hebrew inscriptions in praise of God, of Don Pedro (the Cruel), and of Halevi. Adjacent is the *Sephardic Museum and Library,* set up in 1964 and opened to the public in 1971, containing a number of Jewish tombstones of the 14C, and other relics. Some other Jewish tombs may be seen in the *Museo de Santa Cruz.*

A few minutes walk to the NW brings one to the synagogue of *Santa María la Blanca,* also of Mudéjar workmanship, which was apparently once used as a refuge for reformed prostitutes; as a barrack and storeroom in 1791-98; and later as a carpenter's workshop, but it has since been well restored. The interior has double aisles, separated by octagonal piers with elaborate capitals moulded in plaster and ornamenteed with fir-cone etc. Above are Moorish arches. On the bases of some of the columns, the altar steps, and the pavements, are ancient *azulejos* or tiles. The door and ceiling are of larchwood. The sanctuary dates from c. 1550.

A short distance from El Tránsito stands the so-called *Casa del Greco,* on the site of the old palace of Halevi, replaced by several others before the present structure was erected at the turn of this century by the Marqués de Vega-Inclán in an attempt to recapture the atmosphere of a 16C Manchego mansion.

An underground passage is said to exist along the outer edge of the Judería, which was supposed to be used by both Jews and Marranos to escape persecution.

There must have existed more than one Jewish cemetery. One of importance is that located at the *Cerro de la Horca* on the road to the present-day Christian cemetery behind the Instituto de Enseñanza Media.

About 30 m E of Santa María la Blanca, the remains have been found of a *mikve,* or ritual bath, probably built in the 14C.

Tortosa (47,200 inhab; 85 km SW of Tarragona), a river-port near the mouth of the Ebro, was one of the first sites in Roman Spain settled by the Jews, and a tombstone inscribed in Hebrew, Latin, and Greek would suggest that this might have been as early as the 6C. The Jewish quarter lay to the W of the town, between the present church of *La Inmaculada* (at the foot of the road ascending to the Parador Nacional) and the *Calle de Remolinos,* further W. A good plunging view of the area may be obtained from the wall of the Parador gardens, once those of the fortress.

The community had strong commercial ties with Barcelona and the French Mediterranean ports. Among its natives in the 10-11Cs were the geographer *Ibraham ibn Yaqub,* but the community only numbered about 30 families. In 1148 it was captured by the Christians under *Ramón Berenguer IV,* count of Barcelona, and the Jewish community was given land and enjoyed certain privileges. It suffered during the persecutions of 1391, in spite of the king's insistence that they should be protected, and many sought safety in the fortress. Others were forcibly baptised or voluntarily became *Conversos,* who in 1393 were prohibited to live in the same area as the remaining Jews or have sexual relations with them. The latter were complelled to wear a distinctive dress and a badge, but four years later these conditions were relaxed.

In 1412, however, the town became the focus of the infamous *Disputation of Tortosa,* which actually commenced in February 1413, and lasted until the end of the following year. This was the most important of the Christian-Jewish disputations,

prompted by *Jerónimo de Santa Fe* (himself an apostate, previously known an *Joshua Halorki*), in which he claimed to prove the authenticity of the messianism of Jesus from Jewish sources. *Benedict XIII*, the participating Spanish anti-pope, ordered that the Jewish communities of Aragón and Catalonia should send delegates to Tortosa to argue the case with Jerónimo, and some 69 sessions were held during the next twenty months. The Tortosa community itself was represented by the poet *Solomon ben Reuben Bonafed*, but the Jewish disputants were threatened and intimidated, and the discussion was in no way unbiased, Jerónimo contemptuously condemning parts of the Talmud, which he ordered to be obliterated. The arguments were inconclusive, although the Christians had the upper hand, and took the opportunity to convert a number of participants. The Disputation also incited numerous anti-semitic reactions throughout the kingdom, and persecutions intensified. Nevertheless, by 1417 the community of Tortosa had recovered temporarily; but in 1492 they had to accept baptism or expulsion, and the port was a point of embarkation for many Spanish Jews.

A tombstone may be seen in the Dominican convent to the E of and below the citadel.

Trujillo (9400 inhab; 47 km E of Cáceres) had a community, which towards the end of the 13C was the second largest in Extremadura, with the exception of that in Badajoz, both towns lying on the main road between Toledo and Lisbon. But little is known of their activities until in 1480 the Jews and Conversos were segregated into separate districts. The former were allowed to build a new synagogue, but whether this is the one situated behind the W side of the *Calle Tiendas,* leading S from the Plaza Mayor, is uncertain. On application to the Farmacia Gabriel y José Solís, at No 14 in this street, the proprietor will kindly show in a back room the inscribed lintel which was doubtless over the entrance to a synagogue that must have existed on the site of the adjacent sports-goods shop. The inscription is taken from Psalms 118.20.

Recent research points clearly to locating the 1480 Jewish quarter in the area known as *La Rinconada* on the SE corner of the *Plaza Mayor*.

It is highly probable that the Judería occupied the area S of the *Plaza Mayor*, as far as *Calle Hernando Pizarro*.

Tudela (23,400 inhab; 81 km NW of Zaragoza), birthplace of the poets *Yehuda Halevi* (c.1075-after 1140) and *Abraham ibn Ezra* (1089-1164), and the great medieval traveller *Benjamín de Tudela* (1127-73). There was apparently some tension between the Jewish and Muslim community at the time of the reconquest of *Alfonso I el Batallador*, in 1115, possibly owing to their slave-trading propensity. They were mainly occu-

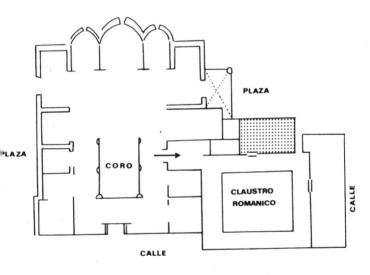

Tudela
  Cathedral and Cloister. Shaded area marks the probable location of the Synagogue.

pied in the textile trades, and as goldsmiths, although the community owned estates and vineyards in the area.

Known as *Mosquera*, the Jewish quarter lay either near the cathedral or in the SE part of the town. Under *Sancho IV of Navarre* (late 12C) they were granted additional privileges, being allocated a cemetery, and allowed to seek safety in the fortress if attacked. It became a haven for co-religionists after their expulsion from France in 1306, but the community suffered sporadically during the 14C, particular during the civil wars of the 1360s. Later in the century *Joseph Orabuena* of Tudela accompanied *Charles III of Navarre* on several journeys as his confidant and physician. There were a number of *Conversos* here prior to 1391, among them the artist *Yojanán de Levi,* after which the community declines, although it was not itself affected during the persecutions of that year. It was further depleted by plague in the 1430s. In 1485 it refused to hand over various Converso fugitives to the Inquisiton after the assassination of *Pedro de Arbués* in the cathedral at Zaragoza. In 1492 some 2000 Jewish refugees from Spain entered this part of Navarre, but they were likewise expelled in 1498. In 1515 a tribunal of the Inquisition was established in Tudela, which carried on its inquiries with renewed ferocity after the Conversos of Navarre rallied to the support of the invading French armies in 1521. A list of those condemned by the Holy Office hung in the cathedral until the close of the 18C.

Various claims have been made as to the site of one of its synagogues, which it is supposed may have abutted the N side of the Romanesque cloister of the *Cathedral,* but there is no documentary evidence for this unlikely position; while the location of the Judería lay to the SE between the cathedral and town wall.

A plaque in honour of Benjamín de Tudela was uncovered some years ago. at No 2 Benjamín de Tudela Street.

Valencia (707,900 inhab; capital of its province) once contained the largest Jewish community in the ancient Kingdom of Valencia, as might be expected. When it was first settled is unknown, but it was already important during the Moslem occupation, largely engaged in tanning, marketing the agricultural produce of its rich *huerta,* and in general commercial activities. *Salomon ibn Gabirol* died here in the late 1050s. By 1238, when it was finally conquered by the Christians, 162 Jewish families resided there. It had previously, in 1095, been briefly occupied by the *Cid,* when a treaty stipulated that Jews were forbidden to acquire Moslem prisoners of war, nor could they be placed in authority over them, etc.

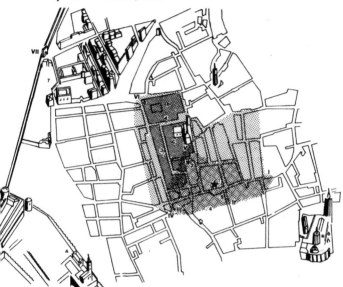

Valencia

> Shaded areas show the locations of the Jewish quarters over the street layout from the 17C.

A. Dominican Convent.
B. Cathedral.
C. Colegio del Patriarca.
D. Old University.

Jewry
I.   La Figuera Square.
II.   La Sabatería Gate.
III. Portal Nou de la Jueria (Jewry New Gate).
IV.   Porta Xarea (Xarea Gate).
V.   Els Cabrerots Square.
VI.   Trebuquet Gate.
VII. Portal dels Jueus (Jews Gate).
1.   Main Synagogue.
2.   Synagogue.
3.   Synagogue.
4.   Jewish Baths.
5.   Jewish Butcher (opp. Synagogue).
6.   Vives family house.
7.   Location of Jewish cemetery.

At this early period the Judería is said to have been in the vicinity of the church of *Santa Catalina*, but it may have been later moved to a position on either side of the present *Calle de la Paz* (with the University at the S corner, *Santa Teresa* at the NE, and the *Palacio de Dos Aguas* just beyond its SW corner). Their cemetery lay in the *Fossar dels Jueus*, which was behind the present *Palacio de Justicia* until built over in 1970.

The community, which had flourished during the late 13C, when the Judería also increased in size, suffered both during and after the Black Death in 1348 and more so in 1391, when Castilian troops awaiting to embark at the port for Sicily, decided to attack the Judería first, in which assault some 250 Jews died. Many fled, while others were converted. In that November a general pardon to the Christian inhabitants of Valencia was issued, to put a stop to further depopulation. The community never fully recovered; despite attempts to strengthen it with settlers from elsewhere.

Vicent Ferrer (1350-1419), born in Valencia, where he professed in 1368, and who gained fame as a preacher in France and elsewhere on the continent, was a virulent anti-semite. Most of the Conversos of Valencia reverted to Judaism, many being apprehended in their attempts to leave the port for the Eastern Mediterranean. The Spanish Inquisition was established there in 1482 (although the Papal Inquisition had been producing a file on Converso activities there since the 1460s). The first Inquisitor, *Cristóbal Gualves*, was removed from his post by Pope *Sixtus IV* in response to numerous complaints of his cruelty, an action which provoked protests from *Fernando of Aragón*. Nevertheless, by 1488 some hundred were burned at the stake, while almost a thousand were reconciled with the Church, and the regional tribunal continued to function sporadically until its abolition early in the 19C.

Several synagogues existed in Valencia: the *Mayor,* later converted into the church of San Cristóbal, located on the *Calle del Mar* between *Calles de Muñoz Degrain* and *Ruiz de Libory;* and the private synagogues of *Ibrahim Morvan* and *Haron Rubio,* behind the Colegio del Patriarca.

Valladolid (286,000 inhab; capital of its province), being an ancient capital of Castile, had an important Jewish community, first mentioned in 1221 although they had settled there during the Moorish occupation.

But the citizens of Valladolid were always reactionary, and the Jews there were prohibited from acquiring land in its vicinity from 1288. In 1322 the municipal council prohibited Christians from attending Jewish or Moorish weddings, and receiving Jewish doctors, while Jews were excluded from holding public office. They were forced to dispute publicly with *Abner of Burgos,* an apostate, in 1336. In 1367, having taken the side of *Enrique de Trastámara* in the civil war, the Jewish quarter was later attacked and its eight synagogues were destroyed. By 1392 the majority of the surviving community had been converted, while the antisemitic *Laws of Valladolid* were promulgated in 1412 under the influence of *Vicent Ferrer.*

Attempts were later made to resuscitate the community, and a new synagogue was the scene of a meeting of delegates from other Jewish communities in Castile intent on their further organisation in 1432 under the leadership of Rab *Abraham Beneveniste* and again in 1476.

In 1486 the Catholic Kings took their part against decisions of the municipal council, but within another six years the surviving members were expelled. The tribunal of the Inquisition here came within the jurisdiction of that of Toledo in 1560. No remains of the Judería are to be seen.

Vic (previously *Vich;* 27,600 inhab; 66 km N of Barcelona) had a community of 40 families in the mid 13C (perhaps descendants of a garrison established there in the early 9C), but later this dwindled in size. Few survived the massacre of 1391, and they converted. The Judería, with its synagogue of 1277, lay between the apse of the *Cathedral* and the *Castillo de Moncada*, centred on the *Plaza d'en Guíu;* while their cemetery lay on the outskirts, in a place called *Colldasens* or *Puig dels Jueus.* In the

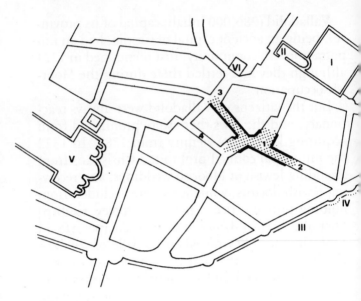

Vic
I. *Moncada Castle.*
II. *Church of San Sadurní.*
III. *Old Wall.*
IV. *Moncada Gate.*
V. *Cathedral.*
VI. *Godina Tower.*
1. *En Guín Square.*
2. *Calcinera Street.*
3. *Baixada de l'Eraime (Eraime Hill).*
4. *Vergós Street.*

Museum is a retablo painted by *Juan* (Yojanán) *de Levi*, four scenes from the Life of St Peter; it probably came from Calatayud.

Vitoria (169,800 inhab; capital of the Basque province of Alava). The Judería lay on the E side of the old centre, but little is known of the community in earlier centuries, which was granted a charter as late as 1488, which briefly protected them from the anti-semitic decrees of 1480. In 1492 its Jews moved into Navarre, and its Conversos were scattered throughout the town in order that their assimilation might be more rapid. The synagogue

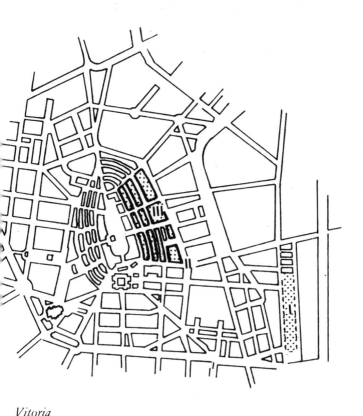

Vitoria
I.   *Judizmendi (Location of old Jewish cemetery).*
II and III. *Location of Jewry.*

was turned into a school, and the cemetery was
given to the town council with the proviso that it
was never built over. This consideration was due
to the fact th the Council asked the Jewish doctors
to defer their departure from the city in order to
attend to victims of the plague then rampant. The
Jewish community agreed on condition that their
cemetery was thereafter preserved. This lay slightly
further E of the S. half of the *Calle Herrán,* and
was long known as *Judizmendi* (Mount of the
Jews). In 1952 the possible descendants of the Jews
of Vitoria, then living in Bayonne (just across the
French frontier), released the present town council from their contract, and the remains were re-
buried in a common grave and a memorial was
erected in a city school —N of Judizmendi Park—
to commemorate the old community.

Zamora (52,000 inhab; capital of its province). Its main Judería, of long standing, lay to the S and W of the present *Parador Nacional* — W as far as the church of *San Ildefonso,* and E as far as the *Plaza Mayor.* Part of it lay without the walls centred on the *Plaza de Santa Lucía,* near the *Puente Viejo* (Old Bridge).

Another Judería lay to the NW of the centre in the district known as *San Lázaro,* together with the Jewish Cementery. It has been claimed that the site

Zamora
I.   *Parador.*
1.   *Santa Lucía Square.*
2.   *Synagogue.*
3.   *Jewish cemetery.*
4.   *Synagogue.*

of one of the synagogues was at No. 15 *Calle Ignacio Gazapo,* a few paces E of the church of *Santa Lucía.*

Certain stones preserving Hebrew letters have been identified in a wall near the *Plaza de Santa Ana,* some distance N of the town centre.

A Church Council held here in 1313 adopted a number of anti-semitic resolutions, including the enforcement of wearing of a distinctive badge. It is not known if they suffered during the persecution of 1391, but in 1491 they were forced to contribute a considerable sum towards the War of Granada, which did not stop them being ejected from the town the following year. Zamora became a transit centre for many thousands of Jews leaving for Portugal, particular for Braganza and Miranda do Douro.

Zaragoza (528,000 inhab; capital of its province) had a Jewish community as early as the late Roman period, and during most of the Middle Ages it was active in tanning, and in the cloth trade. By the 13C it may have numbered 3000. The Judería, which was once walled, and contained two synagogues (one on the site of the church of *San Carlos*; another possibly being *San Andrés*, lay at the SE corner of the old city, bounded to the W by the *Calle de Don Jaime I,* by the *Calle de Coso* to the S and SE, and reaching as far as the *Plaza de María Magdalena,* adjacent to the building of the *Old University.* The *Barrio Nuevo* lay on the S side of the Coso, and contained another synagogue, and *Baths.* The latter is all that now remains of the Judería, which was almost totally destroyed in 1391. They may be visited by applying to the superintendent at No 126-32 in the Coso, for they have been incorporated into the basement of a modern block—which at least «preserves» the relics of the baths, which once covered a larger area.

The city had a large Converso community, among them being *Pedro de la Cavallería,* but many of them suffered under the Inquisition, established in 1484, with its seat in the fortress of *Aljafería,* to the W of the enceinte, particularly after the assassination of *Pedro de Arbués*, one of the inquisitors, which took place in *La Seo*, the old cathedral, on 14 September 1495. From then on autos-de-fe were held monthly, and over 600 Conversos were tried by the tribunal during the next three decades.

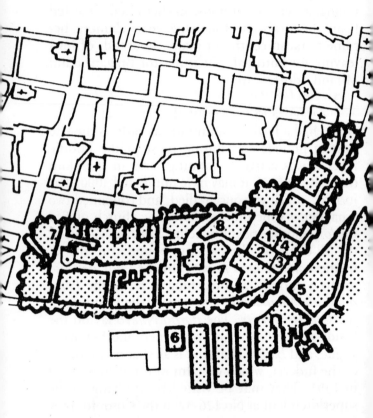

Zaragoza
1. *Jewish hospital.*
2. *Main Synagogue.*
3. *Jewish Butcher.*
4. *Jewish Tower.*
5. *Jewish Bath.*
6. *New Jewry Synagogue.*
7. *Synagogue.*
8. *Talmud Torah.*

OTHER TOWNS

Adra (15,600 inhab; 52 km W of Almería), an ancient port, noted for the Punic inscriptions unearthed there. Here also, in the 18C, was found a marble funerary inscription of the 3C referring to the death of a Jewish girl (Salomonula), and the earliest written reference to the presence of a Jew in the Peninsula. The tablet has since been lost.

Alagón (4800 inhab; 22 km NW of Zaragoza). There was probably a community there prior to its reconquest by the Christians in 1119, and the names of Jewish and Converso notables are recorded in accounts dating from the early 15C; but no relics remain.

Alba de Tormes (4050 inhab; 19 km SE of Salamanca). A charter of 1140 refers to the legal rights of the community, which experienced some slight persecution in 1230. They were also the subject of a satirical 15C play reflecting the prejudices of the period, in which members of the Jewish community brought a suit against a dog that bit them.

Albarracín (2800 inhab; 35 km NW of Teruel) had a Judería in the 12C, and a *fuero* of 1220 regulated their activities. It was affected by the riots of 1391, and in the following year the Judería was entered and many of its inhabitants massacred. Those remaining survived until the expulsion, although their rabbi urged them to leave before conversion was imposed on them. Meanwhile, in 1484-86 a tribunal of the Inquisition operated there, but the deadline date of the expulsion of the Jews was extended a further three months at royal request.

Alcalá de Guadaira (38,700 inhab.; 30 km E of Seville). A synagogue was demolished in 1391 and the church of San Miguel was erected on the site.

Alcañiz (11,000 inhab; 103 km SE of Zaragoza) had a small Jewish community which was protected by the *Infante Martín* during the massacres of 1391, but this later dwindled to a mere 15 families.

Alcolea de Cinca (25 km S of Monzón, province of Huesca). In 1320 Jews were given special privileges for settling there, including the exemption from certain taxes, but the community broke up in 1414.

Almagro (8700 inhab; 23 km SE of Ciudad Real). The Jewish community which had settled there in the 14C grew in the 15C, in the 1460s founding a synagogue, of which there are no remains. They included a number of Conversos from Ciudad Real, who had taken refuge there after the persecutions of 1449, 1469, and 1474.

Almería (120,100 inhab; capital of its province) had an important Jewish community from the late 10C, with its Judería between the Alcazaba and the harbour, but although it survived the Almohad persecutions of the mid 12C and were granted the same protection as the Moors when eventually captured by the Christians in 1488, they were forced into exile after the edict of expulsion of 1492, many sailing to North Africa.

Arévalo (6100 inhab.; 60 km NW of Segovia). Local historians estimate the number of Jews expelled in 1492 at 4000. The approximate location of the last Judería was the area bound by the *Adaja* river and the *Arrabal, Salvador,* and *San Juan de Dios* streets.

Badajoz (102,800 inhab; capital of its province) had a community of Jews trading there in the 11C. It was finally reconquered in 1229, and there are references to the Jews having to pay taxes not long after. Little is known of the community until 1480, when their segregation from Conversos was ordered. In 1492 it was on one of the main routes from Spain into adjacent Portugal.

The Inquisition was active there in 1493-99, when 231 New Christians were punished. In 1535 *David Reubeni* was burned at an auto-de-fe; while a century later a large group of Marranos was detected there, although most of them escaped persecution only by fleeing across the frontier. The location of the Judería is not known.

Balaguer (12,200 inhab; 28 km NE of Lérida). Little is known of the community which had settled there by the 11C, until its persecution after the Black Death (1348-49), but it revived under the patronage of the Counts of Urgell. In 1391 they were refused the protection of the citadel, and those who remained there were further impoverished by the conversions which took place after the Disputation of Tortosa. No remains of the Judería are extant.

Baza (20,100 inhab; 105 km NE of Granada) was annexed to Granada in c.1039, after its capture from Almería by an army lead by *Samuel ibn Joseph ha-Nagid*. Its Jewish community were largely employed in the silk industry, and the Judería lay near the church of *Santiago*. Although some 11C *Arab Baths* have been uncovered, the *Jewish Baths*, after being put to a variety of uses, were totally destroyed as recently as 1907.

Brihuega (45,000 inhab.; 30 km E of Guadalajara). Branching off the main street is the *Calle de la Sinagoga*. In the newer part of the same street, called *Don Rafael San Miguel,* there are some comparatively modern houses, but it is very likely that they were built on the location of at least one synagogue.

Briviesca (4600 inhab; 40 km NE of Burgos). Closely associated with the communities of Burgos and Miranda de Ebro, the Jews of Briviesca were virtually annihilated during the civil wars of the 1360s. Although re-established soon after, their tax-farming activities provoked a series of anti-semitic restrictions promulgated by the Cortes convened there in 1387. Some Jewish residents sold their lands to the monastery of *Oña* —some distance to the N— in 1414, and they were later dispersed.

Burriana (23,900 inhab; 11 km S of Castellón de la Plana), together with adjacent *Villarreal* (36,600 inhab) were important Jewish settlements in the mid 13C, and *Jaime II* made land available to the community for the establishment of a cemetery. Although they recovered to some extent after the troubles of 1391, looted property being restored to them, most of the Jews of Burriana sailed into exile in 1492.

Cádiz (140,900 inhab; capital of its province). Little is known of the community here. The Conversos were rigorously handled by the Inquisition of Seville in 1481. Eleven years later some 8000 Jews (according to *Bernáldez*, the chronicler) left Cádiz for North Africa.

Canary Islands. The first Jewish immigrants are said to be Conversos taking refuge from the Inquisition. Some were summoned to appear before the tribunal at Seville in 1502; others were tried at Córdoba. A number of autos-de-fe were held in the Canaries in 1510, and the activities of the Inquisition were resumed there in 1523-32, and 1568. In the 17C a number of Conversos, many from Portugal, settled in *Palma* and *Tenerife,* some few of which were interrogated in the following century, but without serious consequences.

Cartagena (155,200 inhab; 49 km S of Murcia). This ancient port is referred to in the Talmud and Midrash to denote Spain as a whole, but although presumably having a Jewish community for some centuries previously, this is not mentioned in any detail until the 13C, after its re-conquest. In 1453 and 1462 respectively the tithes of the bishopric were farmed by *Samuel Aventuriel* and *David aben Alfacar*. A tribunal of the Inquisition was established here in 1500. The port had served as a place of embarkation for exiles during the previous decade, some of whom may have remained as Conversos.

Castellón de la Plana (108,650 inhab; capital of its province) had a prosperous Jewish community after its reconquest in 1233, and in 1320 land was acquired for its cemetery. The place was resettled after the pogrom of 1391, a street being allocated for their residence.

Castrojeriz (1200 inhab; 46 km W of Burgos) was one of the earliest Jewish settlements in Spain, being referred to in 974, but little is known of the declining community in later centuries.

Cea (750 inhab; 10 km N of Sahagún, province of León) had a Jewish quarter first mentioned in 1110, most of the inhabitants of which gained a living off agriculture, but little is known of the community in succeeding centuries.

Coca (2100 inhab; 50 km NW of Segovia) had a small community, mentioned in the 13C, but little else is known of it, although it gained a certain notoriety in 1320 when a local Jewess produced an illegitimate child, the father of which was Christian. A Jewish courtier was allowed to judge her by Jewish law, and accordingly her nose was cut off, an action which it was thought might deter others from behaving likewise.

Cuenca (36,800 inhab; capital of its province). Reconquered in 1177, Cuenca was shortly after granted a charter *(fuero)* in which it allowed Jews to settle and trade freely, although they were restricted from taking certain public positions; and fornicating with Christian women was prohibited on pain of burning. The Judería lay near the *Cath-*

edral, and by the late 13C contained between 50-100 families, but in 1391 it was totally destroyed. There was a partial recovery in the 15C, when there were numerous Conversos in the town, but they suffered considerably during the repressive measures adopted by the Inquisition there in 1489. Some of those exiled found their way to Turkey, where they took on the name Cuenca (Kuenka) as their family name.

Dueñas (3100 inhab; 15 km S of Palencia). Its small but flourishing agricultural community suffered losses in the Black Death of 1348-49. Prior to their expulsion in 1492 it is said that the local Old Christians presented them with claims dating back for generations.

Elvira (*Illiberis:* believed to be about 3 km from Granada) was the site of church councils in the early 4C (313-c.317), which issued edicts —the first of their kind in Spain— forbidding the marriage of Jews with Christian women unless first adopting Christianity; forbidding the keeping of Christian concubines; the entertaining of Christians at their table, and the blessing of fields belonging to Christians, etc. The Jewish community there later merged with that of Granada. These various regulations have been considered as the first round in the struggle between Christians and Jews in the accumulation of souls.

Fraga (10,600 inhab; 25 km W of Lléida), the community of which was referred to in the 13C, had its privileges confirmed in 1327-36 by *Alfonso IV.* In 1380 there were some 80 families living there, but many emigrated or were converted after the synagogue was destroyed in 1391; others converted in 1414. In 1436 *Juan I* permitted Jews in the area to establish a new settlement at Fraga, but many Jews remaining there in 1492 were unconditionally expelled.

Haro (8600 inhab; 43 km SW of Vitoria) at one time had a small but prosperous community involved in agriculture, viticulture, and in the manufacture of pottery, etc., but the site of the Judería is not known with any certainty, although it has been assumed that it was in a higher part of the town known as *La Mota*.

Herrera de Pisuerga (3350 inhab; 72 km NE of Palencia) was noted for the persecutions of its Converso community in the 15C, particularly of the female followers of a certain *Inés de Herrera*, who had visions with repect to the fate of the Conversos (who were to be alloted a special place in Heaven for the sufferings they had experienced on Earth). On 1501 some hundred of these women were burned at Toledo in autos-de-fe.

Huete (2850 inhab; 14 km N of Carrascosa del Campo, which is 56 km W of Cuenca), the ancient *Istonium*, contained a prosperous Jewish community in the 13C, and after 1391 it harboured some Conversos. They were punished for demonstrating against their expulsion in 1492.

Illescas (4900 inhab; 36 km SW of Madrid). The community had vineyards and olive-groves prior to 1342, when the archbishop of Toledo confiscated them on the grounds that they had been acquired illegally. The Jews there were attacked in 1391, and in 1492 were robbed by those they had hired for their protection while en route to Cartagena and Morocco. Its many Conversos were subsequently tried by the Inquisition.

Jaén (82,050 inhab; capital of its province) had a community during the early part of the Muslim era until the Almohad persecutions, among whom was the father of Hasdai ibn Shaprut, who later moved to Córdoba. The town was captured by the Christians in 1246. In 1360s it was taken by the Muslims of Granada, allied to *Pedro the Cruel*, who were allowed to sell the Jews —some 300 families— as slaves. A riot against its Conversos broke out in 1473, and a decade later its Jews were expelled. A tribunal of the Inquisition was temporarily established here, and carried out its work sporadically until amalgamating with that of Córdoba in 1526.

Llerena (5200 inhab; 95 km SE of Mérida, off the road from Zafra to Córdoba) had a Jewish community in the 13-15Cs, among them *Gabriel Israel,* who served as an interpreter to Fernando and Isabel during the Wars of Granada. A tribunal of the Inquisition was later set up there, and was officiously active well into the first half of the 17C.

Maqueda (a small village 74 km SW of Madrid, and 42 km NW of Toledo), probably had a community from the late 12C. Its two synagogues were sacked in 1391, but the community survived, and it was here in 1430 that *Moses Arragel* completed his translation of the Bible into Castilian, having been commissioned to do so by *Luis de Guzmán,* head of the Order of Calatrava. Its importance may be gauged by the fact that representatives of the Jewish communities throughout Castile were convened there in 1484.

Murcia (262,100 inhab; capital of its province) had an important community prior to the reconquest of the kingdom, and Jewish officials continued to hold positions of responsability there although *Alfonso X* of Castile insisted that they should forthwith live separated from Christians, allocating to them a sector of the town and a cemetery. In 1307 jurisdiction over the Muslims of the kingdom of Murcia was entrusted to *Isaac ibn Yaish,* the last Jew to hold such a post. In general they lived without friction with the Christian residents, and in the 15C provided a number of tax-farmers both in Murcia and further afield. It is presumed that in 1492 the Jews sailed hence from neighbouring Cartagena.

Orihuela (48,100 inhab; 25 km NE of Murcia) had a community when captured by *Alfonso X,* but virtually all of them accepted baptism during the troubles of 1391.

Sahagún (2600 inhab; 66 km SE of León) had a small Judería of c.30 families who from the early 10C lived near the influencial monastery here, on which they were partially dependent. The area of this quarter lay to the N of the centre, and was known as *Santa Cruz,* but no identifiable relics of the community survive.

Santa Coloma de Queralt (2800 inhab; 30 km NE of Montblanch, province of Tarragona) had a small but thriving community which lived in the district known as the *Carrer de los Quarteres.* It was known in the late 14C for its «lady doctor», *Na Floreta Canoga,* a Jewess who was well-considered at the Aragonese court. It is not known whether the community survived for long after the conversions precipitated by the Disputation of Tortosa (1414).

Segorbe (7300 inhab; c.54 km N of Valencia). Little is known of this community, which was resident there after its reconquest by the Christians, and it is possible that early in the 15C it may have moved to neighbouring *Murviedro (Sagunto;* see p. 68).

Talavera de la Reina (56,000 inhab; 117 km SW of Madrid) had a small community of Jews dependent on Toledo, and after 1449 many Jews from the capital moved there in an attempt to evade persecution. Some 170 families resided there in the 1480s. The Inquisition of Toledo caught up with them, and a number were sentenced to expulsion, to be followed in 1492 by any others who had not been baptised meanwhile.

Tárrega (10,600 inhab; 44 km E of Lléida) had a properous community prior to the 13C, but it suffered in persecutions during the period of the Black Death (1348-49), when some 300 Jews were said to have been slaughtered. Orders to rebuild the Jewish quarter were issued in 1350 at a place called *La Font.* It appears that a new synagogue had been erected in 1346, just prior to the riots.

Little else is known of the community during the following century and a half.

Valmaseda (7900 inhab; 29 km SW of Bilbao) had a community in the 15C, who settled near the old bridge in the *San Lorenzo* quarter, but pressure was brought against them in 1483 by local guilds, and in 1486 their expulsion from the area was decreed. Their voluntary departure took place the following year.

Vilafranca del Penedès (prev. Villafranca del Panades; 20,200 inhab; 48 km W of Barcelona) had a community early in the 12C, partly of French origin. It was protected against communal rioting after the Black Death in 1348, and again in 1353, but does not appear to have survived the pogrom of 1391.

BIOGRAPHICAL NOTES

Eminent Jews in medieval Spain

Abarbanel (or *Abravanel*), *Isaac* (1437-1508), born in Lisbon, was the author of commentaries on the Kabbala, among other works. He was also treasurer successively to the kings of Portugal, Spain, and Naples, but his offer to Fernando V of 30,000 ducats to prevent the expulsion of the Jews in 1492 was in vain.

Abarbanel, Judah (c.1460-c.1521), son of the above, and also known as *León Hebreo,* was born in Lisbon. He wrote some neo-Platonic *Dialoghi d'amore* in Italy, and his ideas, much indebted to the Hispano-Jewish tradition, influenced a number of Renaissance writers, including Bembo and Castiglione, among others. He lived as a physician in Genoa and Naples, where he died.

Abu 'l-Afia, Abraham ben Samuel (1240-91), a famous kabbalist, born in Zaragoza, whence he moved to Tudela before setting out on a pilgrimage to Israel. He had returned to Barcelona by 1271, but left Spain two years later. He completed his most influential mystical work, the *Imrei Shefer* in the year of his death.

Abu 'l-Afia, Meir (c.1170-1244), one of the most distinguished rabbis and Talmudic scholars of his epoch, who spent most of his life in Toledo. He is best known for his controversy with Maimonides, whose doctrine of resurrection he considered heretical. Nevertheless, he held Maimonides in great esteem, and wrote an elegy on his death.

Abu 'l-Afia, Todros ben Yehuda (1247-c.1303), Hebrew poet, born in Toledo, who enjoyed the patronage of Alfonso X. He wrote a great quantity of verse, much of it of slender merit, at first licentious in tone, later almost religious, which gives some insight into the period.

Adret, Salomon ben (1235-c.1310), born in Barcelona, was Chief Rabbi of Spain and an authority on Spanish-Hebrew law and religion, who wrote numerous kabbalistic works, responsa, etc.

Albo, Joseph (c.1380-1444), Spanish Hebrew philosopher, who in his *Sefer ha-'iqqarim* («Fundamentals of the Faith») continued the tradition of his master Hasdai Crescas. He defended the Talmud at the Disputation of Tortosa in 1413.

Alfasi, Isaac ben Jacob (1013-1103), born in North Africa, after a period of study in Kairouan, settled in Fez, where he remained until 1088, in the following year moving (via Córdoba, briefly) to Lucena, where he died. Among his students there were Ibn Migash, Yehudah Halevi, and Ibn Gabirol. His death was mourned in poems by Moses ibn Ezra, for he was one the foremost Talmudic scholars of the time, famous especially for his *Sefer ha-halahot* (first published in Constantinople in 1509), an epitome of the Talmud, which thereby facilitated its study. He was greatly admired by Maimonides, amongst others, and established in Lucena one of the first Talmudic centres in Western Europe, a true successor to the Talmudic Academies of Sura and Pumbedita.

Arragel, Moses, 15C scholar, born in Guadalajara, settled in Maqueda in 1422 at the invitation of Luis de Guzmán, Grand Master of Calatrava, to translate the Bible into Castilian, which was completed in 1433 together with a commentary. He was assisted in his task by Franciscans from Toledo.

Asher ben Yehiel (c. 1250-1327), born in Cologne, and died at Toledo, was one of the most influential rabbinic leaders of his time, taking up the post of rabbi in Toledo in 1305. His halakhic works are modelled on those of Alfasi, and they number over 1000 responsa.

Benveniste, Abraham (1406-54 or 66), a native of Soria, Benveniste was an influential «court rabbi» and tax-farmer under Juan II. In 1432 he convened representatives of the Castilian Jewish communities at Valladolid to frame a series of ordinances to protect and strengthen their much undermined position.

Benjamín of Tudela (Benjamín ben Jonah; second half of 12C). Little is known of this famous medieval Jewish traveller except from what emerges from his *Sefer ha-massa'ot* or *Itinerary* of his travels. It is uncertain exactly when he set out from Spain, but be returned there in 1172/3 from Egypt. His travels took him through Provence and Italy, and then through Greece to Constantinople. He continued by sea via Cyprus to Israel; thence to Bagdad, etc. He probably returned by sea via Sicily to Spain.

Caro, Joseph ben Ephraim (1488-1575), born in Toledo. At an early age his family left for Portugal and then Turkey (from 1497), where he resided for about 40 years. He died in Safed. He is famous for his *Beit Yosef* (completed in 1542, and for his authoritative *Shulhan Arukh,* a code of Orthodox Jewish law. He showed great admiration for Maimonides, and it has been estimated that one third of his work is copied verbatim from him.

Cavallería (or *Caballería*), *Judah de la* (d. 1276), bailiff of Zaragoza by 1257, where he held a privileged position financing the construction of a fleet, and during the Murcia campaign the garrisoning of fortresses south of Valencia, of which he was also appointed bailiff.

Crescas, Hasdai (1340-1410), Born in Barcelona, in c. 1388 he settled in Zaragoza, as Chief Rabbi of Aragón, and he was there during the progrom of 1391, in which his only son was killed (in Barcelona). During the following decade he was active in endeavouring to rehabilitate Spanish Jewry. He also wrote a history of the Aragonese pogrom, but his major work is *Or Adonai,* an anti-Aristotelian classic, first published in Ferrara in 1555, in which although he praised Maimonides learning and intentions, he refuted most of his propositions and proofs, etc., thereby contributing to the growth of Renaissance philosophy.

Cresques, Abraham (d. 1387) and his son *Judah* (born c. 1360) were eminent Catalan cartographers (in fact from Majorca), who enjoyed the special protection and encouragement of Pedro IV of Aragón and his son, later Juan I. Their map of the known world —known as the «Catalan Atlas» —was sent as a gift to Charles VI of France in 1381. Judah converted in 1391, taking the name *Jaime Ribes*, and in 1394 settled in Barcelona. He was also collaborating with Henry the Navigator of Portugal during the 1420s.

Daud, Abraham ben David ha-Levi ibn (c. 1110-80). Born in Córdoba, he later moved to Toledo, where his major historical work —*Sefer ha-Kabbalah*— was written, which had considerable influence in later centuries.

Duran, Simeon ben Zemah (1361-1444), a rabbinic authority, born in Majorca, who left for Algiers in 1391. He was a prolific writer on numerous subjects, and also a poet. His most important philosophical treatise was his *Magen Avot*.

His son, *Soloman ben Simeon Duran* (c. 1400-67), born in Algiers, attacked the apostate Jerónimo de Santa Fe in his apologetical *Milhemet Mitzrah* (1438).

Ezra, Abraham ben Meir ibn (1089-1164). Born in Tudela, as was his friend Yehudah Halevi, he spent the first part of his life in Spain, although he may have visited North Africa; while in 1140 he left Spain for Rome, and during the last years of his life continued to travel in Italy, France, and to London. He wrote much on mathematics, and astronomy, and his biblical commentaries were widely used and respected; he also wrote poetry.

Ezra, Moses ben Jacob ibn (c. 1055-c. 1138). Born in Granada into a wealthy family, he started writing poetry in his youth. He may have visited Lucena to study under Ishaq Gayyat, and later befriended his younger contemporary Yehudah Halevi. He was forced to leave Granada soon after the Almoravide invasion of 1090, and escaped into Christian Spain. Apart from being a prolific poet, he was also author of a treatise on poetry and rhetoric, written after 1135.

Ferruziel, Joseph (also known as *Cidellus*), physician and minister to Alfonso VI, and protector of the Hebrew conmunity in Castile.

Gabirol, Salomon ben Judah ibn (c. 1021-c. 1057; also known as *Avicebron*), philosopher and poet, born in Málaga, whose most famous work, translated into Latin, was *Fons vitae,* passing on the Plotinian and neo-Platonic tradition. It is said to have influenced Aquinus, Duns Scotus, and Ramón Llull.

Gayyat, Ishaq ben (1038-89) was one of the most important talmudists of Lucena, his birthplace, under whose leadership the place became a centre of Western European Jewish scholarship. He was a prolific commentator on the Talmud (in Arabic), but also composed some poetry. He was a friend of both the Ibn Ezra family and of Yehudah Halevi.

Halevi, Yehudah (c. 1075-c. 1141), possibly born in Tudela and educated in Granada, he was one of the most eminent poets of his time writing in Hebrew, and was a friend of many of his contemporary poets in al-Andalus. He later resided in Toledo, before wandering abroad, and he died either in Egypt or in Israel. Between 1130-40 he composed in Arabic a philosophical treatise as a «proof and defence of the despised religion», in which a controversy between religious systems ends with the vindication of Judaism. Over 800 poems by Halevi are known.

Halevi, Samuel (1320-69), treasurer to Pedro I of Castile, and builder of the Tránsito synagogue at Toledo.

Labrat, Dunash ha-Levi ben (c. 920-980), after studying in Bagdad and Fez, became a protegé of Hasdai ben Shaprut in Córdoba. He is responsible for introducing into Spain the new science of Hebrew grammar, demonstrating how easily Hebrew poetry could be composed in the style of classical Arabic poetry. His religious poems are the first of their type by a Jewish writer to have survived in Spain.

Maimonides, Moses (1135-1204). Born in Córdoba, Maimonides is considered one of the most eminent and influential of Spanish Jewish philosophers, although he and his family left for Fez when he was aged 16, having been obliged to leave Córdoba itself as a result of the Almohad persecutions (1148), by which time the family had become «formally» converted to Islam. He later lived in Acre, Jerusalem, and Hebron, before settling in Alexandria as Chief Rabbi; and from 1185 as physician to the Sultan at Cairo (for whom in 1198 he compiled a «Guide to Good Health»). Maimonides died at Fostat, and was buried in Tiberias, where his grave is still the object of pilgrimage.

His most important works are commentaries on the Mishnah (1168); the *Mishneh Torah* (1180; the finest of all medieval expositions of Jewish law); and particularly his «Guide to the perplexed», the *Dalalat al-ha'irin,* translated into Hebrew c. 1204 as *Moreh nevukhim.* They aroused some criticism among the more traditional or dogmatic Jews, but they had a lasting influence on Spinoza, Moses Mendelssohn, and more recent Jewish philosophers; while among medieval Christian writers who were acquainted with his work may be numbered Albertus Magnus, Aquinus, Duns Scotus, and Meister Eckhart, etc.

Maleha, Zac (Isaac) de la, administrator of taxation under Alfonso X.

Migash, Joseph ben Meir ha-Levi ibn (1077-1141), born in Seville and dying at Lucena, he was one of the greatest Spanish talmudic scholars, enjoying a considerable reputation amongst his contemporaries, including the father of Maimonides. He studied for 12 years under Alfasi; Yehudah Halevi composed poems in his praise, but little of his work is extant. His commentaries on the Talmud were incorporated in the work of Meir Abu'l-Afia and Nahmanides, and influenced a wider circle.

Moses ben Shem Tov de León (c. 1240-1305), an influential kabbalist usually known as *Moses de León,* and the compiler of the *Sefer Ha-Zohar.*

Nagrella, Shemuel ha-Levi ben Yosef ibn (993-1056), also known as *Ha-Nagid,* the prince, poet, statesman, and general, was probably born in Mérida and educated in Córdoba, settling in Málaga when the former city was sacked by the Berbers in 1013. He became secretary to the vizier there, and to the King of Granada in 1025. Two year later he was appointed vizier of Granada, and later commander-in-chief, leading his forces against Seville, Carmona, and Almería (1038-56). He was also a patron of learning, and assisted Ibn Gabirol after his banishment from Zaragoza. His own poetic output was extensive, but he also wrote on the art of war, politics, and Hebrew grammar, and commentaries on the Talmud.

Nahmanides (Moses ben Nahman; 1194-1270), one of the leading talmudic scholars, was born at Girona. His Spanish name was *Bonastrug da Porta.* He attempted to fine a compromise between opposing camps during the Maimonides controversy. His opinions were sought by Jaime I of Aragón, who organised a public disputation at Barcelona with Pablo Cristiani, an apostate, in which Nahmanides gained the prize, although the Dominicans endeavoured to bring him to trial in spite of royal support, and he was obliged to flee the country, emigrating to Israel (1267) where he died, but his tomb is not known. His halakhic writings in particular had a decisive influence on subsequent rabbinic literature, and even Salomon ben Abraham ben Adret's glosses on the Talmud are extracted from his work.

Paquda, Bahya ben Joseph ibn (fl. 1050-1100). An influential moral philosopher, probably a resident of Zaragoza. His major work, *Hovot ha-Levevot* («Duties of the Heart») is modelled on works of Moslem mysticism, but his teaching remain in the line of Jewish tradition.

Perfet, Isaac ben Sheshet, an influential rabbinic authority, was born in Barcelona in 1326.

Santob de Carrión or *Shem Tov Ardutiel* (c. 1290-1369), rabbi of Carrion de los Condes, and poet, whose *Proverbios morales* (c. 1355-60), drawn from biblical and talmudic sources, and dedicated to Pedro I of Castile, enjoyed considerable popularity and were later imitated by the Marqués de Santillana, among others. One of the manuscripts was written in Spanish in Hebrew characters.

Seneor, Abraham (also *Senior;* c. 1412-c. 1493) was one of the more prominent and influential courtiers during the reigns of Enrique IV and the Catholic Kings, for both of whom he acted as tax-farmer. He enjoyed the special protection of the latter in gratitude for his personal services prior to their proclamation as rulers, and he was allocated a pension for life from 1475. In 1488 he was appointed treasurer to the Hermandad. He did much to assist Jewish communities in Spain at a crucial time in its history, and after the capture of Málaga in 1487 he directed his efforts to redeem the Jewish captives. He was also largely responsible for the financing of the Granada Campaign, but in 1492, in the face of pressure from Fernando and Isabel, he finally converted to Christianity at a ceremony at Guadalupe, when he changed his name to *Fernando Núñez Coronel.* He was then appointed *regidor* of Segovia —his home town— among other offices, and became a member of the royal council.

Shaprut, Hasdai ben (915-968/78), born in Jaén, and a great scholar and humanist. He had a wide knowledge of languages, and was both a physician, botanist, and diplomat. He was Latin secretary and later minister to Abderahman III at Córdoba, where he died. He cured Sancho the Fat of Navarre of an illness, which did much to increase his reputation.

Shem Tov, Joseph ibn (c. 1400-c. 1460), a philosopher and physician at the Castilian court of Juan II and Enrique IV, who sent him to Segovia in 1452 in an endeavour to suppress an anti-semitic movement. He wrote a number of commentaries on Aristotle and Averroes, but his major work is the *Kevod Elohim,* composed in 1442, in which he compares Aristotelian and Jewish conceptions of the greatest good, etc. It was widely read and influenced later dogmatic and speculative Hebrew literature.

Verga, Salomon ibn (fl. late 15th and early 16C), Jewish historiographer, whose *Shevet Yehudah* (first published in 1554) is an account of the persecutions experienced by the Jews from the destruction of the Second Temple to his own time, but his approach to the subject is critical and empirical. In 1492 he settled in Lisbon, and in 1506 moved to Italy.

Waqar, Isaac and *Abraham ibn,* two eminent members of a family of physicians, both in the service of Sancho IV of Castile (1284-95). In the following century *Joseph ibn Waqar* was physician to Enrique II (1369-79), for whom he travelled to Granada on a diplomatic mission; he also composed an epitome of the history of Spanish kings.

Zacut, Abraham ben Samuel (1452-c. 1515), astronomer and historian, attended the University of Salamanca, and there wrote his major treatise in 1473/78, entitled *Ha-Hibbur ha-Gadol,* which was translated into Latin under the title *Almanach perpetuum celestium motuum.* He emigrated to Portugal in 1492 and became court astronomer to João II and Manuel I, until the expulsion of Jews from Portugal in 1497. He was also the author of a book on genealogies, *Sefer ha-Yuhasin* (completed in 1504 at Tunis). He later travelled to Jerusalem and Damascus.

Conversos and descendants of Conversos

Among the more eminent Conversos of Spain were:

Petrus Alfonsi (Pedro Alfonso; 1062-c. 1110), as he is usually known, from the name he assumed after his conversion at the age of 44, was born at Huesca. He was the author of a collection of tales, mainly from Arabic sources, entitled *Disciplina clericalis,* and a polemical treatise defending his conversion. The second half of his life was spent in England, where he became physician to Henry I.

Cavallería (or *Caballería*), *Pedro de la* (c. 1415-c. 1461), comptroller-general of Aragón and adviser to Alfonso V. He wrote an anti-Jewish polemic in 1450 in which he shows his considerable knowledge of Hebrew literature.

Cristiano, Pablo, a 13C Converso, who entered the Dominican Order, and became involved in controversy with Moses de Gerona in 1263.

Halorki, Joshuah, talmudist and Converso at the court of Benedict XIII, the anti-pope, was a native of Lorca. He changed his name to *Jerónimo de Santa Fé,* and wrote a number of anti-semitic tracts. In 1413-14 he took part in the Disputation of Tortosa, being one of the main Christian contenders in the controversy.

Santa María, Pablo García de (Salomon Halevi; c. 1350-1435), born in Burgos, was possibly baptised in 1390 or during the riots of the following year. He travelled to Paris and was ordained priest, before settling at Avignon, where he became a favourite of Benedict XIII. His ascent in the Catholic hierarchy was rapid. By 1401 he was Bishop of Cartagena, and from 1415-35 Bishop of Burgos. His son, *Alfonso de (Santa María de) Cartagena* (1384-1456) succeeded him as bishop at Burgos, and wrote in defence of the Conversos, among many other works.

Valladolid, Alfonso de (also known as *Abner of Burgos;* c. 1270-c. 1350), a Converso from 1321, who wrote virulently against his previous co-religionists.

Valladolid, Juan de (1403-1452), a blind poet known for his *Coplas de Juan Poeta,* satirising the Manrique family, with whom he had a running battle. He spent some years in Italy, and was held for ransom at Fez after his capture by Barbary pirates.

The **descendants of Conversos** were influential out of all proportion to their numbers; indeed the culture of 16-17C Spain would be very much the poorer without them. Among them were such figures as:

Juan de la Cruz, San (St. John of the Cross; 1542-91), born *Juan de Yepes y Alvarez,* at Fontiveros, near Avila, of probably (but unproven) Converso lineage, his father having been brought up by uncles who were wealthy silk merchants at Toledo. He studied at Salamanca before becoming spiritual director at Santa Teresa's convent at Avila, after which he was active in the Carmelite reform movement. He was jailed in Toledo in 1577 for almost nine months, during which time he composed some of his great mystical poems.

Luis de León (1527-91), born at Belmonte (province of Cuenca) had a Jewish great-grandmother. After studying at Salamanca, where he was brilliant scholar, he commenced translating the «Song of Songs» among other works, and criticised the Vulgate, for which in 1572 he was confined by the Inquisition until 1576, when he was pronounced innocent. He is now read mostly for his poetry.

Teresa de Avila, Santa (1515-82), born *Teresa Sánchez de Cepeda y Ahumada* into a family of Converso lineage (her grandfather being a silk merchant at Toledo, which he left for Avila in 1465). Together with San Juan de la Cruz (see above) she set out to reform the Carmelite Order, reforming or establishing some 32 convents throughout Spain. Her «Autobiography» was denounced by the Inquisition, and she was confined at Toledo, where she wrote *Las moradas,* a milestone of Western spiritual literature.

Vives, Juan Luis (1492-1540), one of the great Renaissance humanists, was born at Valencia of Converso parents, and in 1509 went to study at Paris. In 1512 he moved to Bruges, and in 1517 to Louvain, where he became a close friend of Erasmus. On Nebrija's death (1522) he was offered his chair at Alcalá, but refused it. He spent some years in England, returning to Bruges in 1527.

Others of importance in their various fields were; among poets: *Juan de Mena* (1411-56); *Rodrigo de Cota* (d. after 1504), whose *Epithalamium* alludes to Jewish customs of the period, although he is better known for his *Diálogo entre el amor y un viejo,* first published in the *Cancionero general* of 1511; *Juan Alvarez Gato* (c. 1433-c. 1509); and *Luis de Góngora* (1561-1627) was likewise of Converso descent.

Among chroniclers were *Hernando del Pulgar* (1436-1495), author of the *Libro de los claros varones de Castilla* (Toledo, 1486); *Fernández de Oviedo* (1487-1557); *Diego de Valera* (1412-88); *Andrés Bernaldez* (c. 1450-1513), author of *Historia de los reyes católicos; Fernando de la Torre; Pedro Fernández del Pulgar,* and *Gonzalo de Ayora.*

Among playwrights: *Bartolomé de Torres Naharro* (1485-1524); *Lucas Fernández* (1474-1542); and *Juan de la Encina* (1469-1529).

And among other authors: *Fernando de Rojas* (c. 1465-1541), whose novel written in dramatic form entitled *Comedia de Calisto y Melibea,* better known as *La Celestina* (earliest surviving edition, Burgos 1499) was reprinted at least 60 times in the 16C alone; *Mateo Alemán* (1547-1615), whose picaresque novel *Guzmán de Alfarache* (first part published 1599) began the vogue for this popular literary form; *Juan de Avila* (1500-69), the preacher and religious writer; *Alfonso de Valdés* (1490-1532) and his brother *Juan de Valdés* (c. 1491-1541).

Likewise descended from Conversos were the naturalist, botanist, and physician *Andrés Laguna* (1499-1560); *Antonio de Nebrija* (1444-1522), the humanist and lexicographer; *Arias Montano* (1527-98), the hebraist and first librarian of the Escorial; the jurists *Francisco de Vitoria* (c. 1483-1546), and *Francisco Suárez* (1548-1617); *Luis de Santángel* (d. 1498), tax-collector to the Catholic Kings until 1481, and then appointed comptroller-general (he is also said to have recommended that Columbus receive financial backing); *Miguel Pérez de Almazán,* Secretary of State to *Fernando V* (whose mother, *Juana Enriquez* was of Jewish descent); *Antonio Pérez* (1540-1611), secretary to Philip II; *Diego de Deza* (c. 1443-1523), confessor to Queen Isabel; and even *Tomás de Torquemada* (1420-98), the infamous Dominican Inquisitor-General appointed by the Catholic Kings in 1483 (during whose 18-year control it is estimated that some 2000 heretics —mostly Conversos— were burnt alive, and a further 17,000 mutilated in some way).

Among eminent *Marranos* may be mentioned *Isaac Cardoso* (1604-83), he physician and philosopher; *Menasseh ben Israel,* who in 1627 established the first Hebrew printing-press in Amsterdam; *Joseph* (or *Juan*) *Miges* (or *João Miguez*), also known as *Joseph Nasi* and later created the Duke of Naxos; *Alvaro Mendes,* later Duke of Mitylene; *Gracia Mendes,* previously known as *Beatrice de Luna; Antonio Homen; Antonio Gómez;* the playwright *Antonio Enriquez Gómez;* and *Rodrigo Mendes da Silva,* the historian, among numerous other lesser known figures.

Comunidad Israelita de Madrid
Balmes 3
MADRID 10

(91) 445 95 35
445 98 43

Comunidad Israelita de Barcelona
Porvenir 24
BARCELONA 21

(93) 200 61 48
200 85 13

Comunidad Israelita de Ceuta
Sargento Coriat 8
CEUTA

(956) 51 32 76

Comunidad Israelita de Melilla
General Mola 19
MELILLA

(952) 68 16 00

Comunidad Israelita de Málaga
Duquesa de Parcent 4
MALAGA 1

(952) 21 40 41

Comunidad Israelita de Sevilla
Peral 10
SEVILLA 2

(954) 25 81 00
ext. 324

Sr. Samuel Serfaty
Ausias March 42, Puerta 35
VALENCIA 6

(96) 334 34 16

Sr. Meyer Ohayón
Palmera 20, Urb. El Real
MARBELLA (Málaga)

(952) 77 15 86
77 07 57

Sr. Pinhas Adecasif
Villalba Hervás 3
SANTA CRUZ DE TENERIFE

(922) 24 77 81
24 72 46

Sr. Arnold Spicer
Apartado de Correos 389
PALMA DE MALLORCA

(971) 23 86 86

Sr. Ralph Cohen
Ramón y Cajal 9 - 7º
ALICANTE

Centro de Estudios Judeo-Cristianos
Hilarión Eslava 50
MADRID 15

(91) 243 12 51

Amistad España-Israel
Castellana 45, 3º dcha.
MADRID 1

Beth Minzi
Calle Skal (La Roca)
TORREMOLINOS (Málaga)

(952) 38 39 52

Asociación de Relaciones Culturales
España-Israel
Diputación 237, 5º, 3ª
BARCELONA 7

NOTES